Overfishing:
The Icelandic Solution

Hannes H. Gissurarson

Published by the Institute of Economic Affairs
2000

First published in August 2000
The Institute of Economic Affairs
2 Lord North Street
Westminster
London
SW1P 3LB

Studies on the Environment No.17
ISBN 0-255 36489-X

Printed in Great Britain by
Hartington Fine Arts Limited, Lancing, West Sussex
Set in Times New Roman 11 on 13 point

Contents

Acknowledgements	5
Foreword	**6**
The Author	9
Introduction	10
1.	**The Evolution of the ITQ System**	**12**
	Effort Quotas, 1977-83	13
	The Introduction of Vessel Catch Quotas, 1983-4	15
	A Mixed System, 1985-90	17
	A Comprehensive System of ITQs, 1990	19
	Further Developments in the ITQ System, 1990-2000	22
	Legal Decisions on ITQs	24
	Concluding Remarks	26
2.	**The Nature of the ITQ System**	**29**
	TACs	30
	ITQs	33
	Harvesting Outside Iceland's EEZ	35
	Administration and Enforcement	37
	Are the Icelandic ITQs Property Rights?	39
	Concluding Remarks	41
3.	**The Performance of the ITQ System**	**44**
	The Pelagic and Small Fisheries	45
	The Demersal Fisheries	46
	The Impact on Regional Development	48
	Concentration of ITQs?	52
	Remaining Problems	55

4.	**Current Controversies**	**58**
	Is the ITQ System Unjust?	59
	The Demand For a Resource Rent Tax	61
	Possible Future Developments	63
	References	66
	Summary	*Back Cover*

List of Tables

Table 1: Main Stages in the Evolution of the Icelandic ITQ System

Table 2: Recommended and Set TACs in Cod and Total Actual Catches, 1984-2000

Table 3: TACs in Different Species of Fish for the Fishing Year 1999-2000

Table 4: Catch of Icelandic Vessels Outside Iceland's EEZ, 1994-8

Table 5: Share of Quota Holdings by Regions, 1984-99

Table 6: Share of Demersal Landings by Regions, 1983-98

Table 7: Quota Shares of Largest Harvesting Firms in Demersal Fisheries 1991-99

Table 8: Distribution of Stock in Ten Largest Demersal Harvesting Firms in November 1998

List of Figures

Figure 1: The Icelandic EEZ

Figure 2: Fishing Capital and Catch Values, 1945-97

Figure 3: Catch Per Unit of Fleet in the Pelagic Fisheries, 1977-97

Figure 4: Demersal Fishing Effort and Capital, 1979-97

Figure 5: The Regions of Iceland

List of Common Abbreviations

ACE = Annual Catch Entitlement (multiple of a vessel's TAC-share and the TAC for a given year)

EEZ = Exclusive Economic Zone (200 nautical miles for Iceland since 1975)

FD = Fisheries Directorate in Reykjavik, Iceland

GRT = Gross Registered Tonnes, measuring the volume of a fishing vessel

ITQ = Individual Transferable Quota, shares of each vessel in the TAC (see below)

MRI = Marine Research Institute in Reykjavik, Iceland

MT = Metric Tonnes, measuring the weight of catch

TAC = Total Allowable Catch, set annually for a given fish stock

Acknowledgements

While I am solely responsible for any errors or mistakes found in the following pages, Professors G.S. Becker of the University of Chicago, J.M. Buchanan and H. Manne of George Mason University and H. Demsetz of the University of California at Los Angeles read an earlier draft of what eventually became this paper, all making valuable suggestions. Professors A. Scott of the University of British Columbia, R. Arnason and B.T. Runolfsson of the University of Iceland and R. Hannesson of the Norwegian School of Business Administration in Bergen read the (then considerably longer) first manuscript, also making many corrections and improvements. In numerous discussions, Roger Bate, Roger Beattie, Michael De Alessi, and Julian Morris shared with me their insights into environmental problems in fisheries. The Icelandic Ministry of Fisheries, the Research Fund of the University of Iceland and the Icelandic Science Foundation assisted me in my research. The staff of the Marine Research Institute, the Fisheries Directorate and the National Economic Institute provided me with many facts about the Icelandic economy and the fisheries sector. Finally, Professor E. Colombatto and Ms. A. Calusso provided a stimulating and pleasant environment at the International Centre for Economic Research at Villa Gualino in Turin, where this paper was drafted during a sabbatical from the University of Iceland.

H.H.G.

5

Foreword

In this monograph, Professor Gissurarson provides a very complete historical chronology of the development of individual transferable quotas (ITQs) in Icelandic fisheries. ITQs are the most complete solutions to the problem of the common pool in fisheries. The hazards of open-access fisheries have been understood for a very long time. Indeed, the fishery, unfortunately, has been the best example of depletion and waste associated with unrestricted entry and harvest that is inherent in the 'tragedy of the commons,' as described by Garrett Hardin (1968). Hardin was not the first social scientist to call attention to the losses of the common pool. More than a decade before his article, H. Scott Gordon (1954) outlined a similar logic that was extended by Anthony Scott (1955) and Steven N.S. Cheung (1970). Gordon was concerned about overfishing in the absence of property rights:

> 'There appears then, to be some truth in the conservative dictum that everybody's property is nobody's property. Wealth that is free for all is valued by no one because he who is foolhardy enough to wait for its proper time of use will only find that it has been taken by another . . . The fish in the sea are valueless to the fisherman, because there is no assurance that they will be there for him tomorrow if they are left behind today' (Gordon 1954, 124).

Under the common pool, each fisher considers only his private net benefits while ignoring broader social costs. There is too rapid and intensive harvest, over-capitalization, under-investment in the stock, and ultimately depletion. Under these conditions, societies and communities dependent upon fisheries for their livelihoods are at risk. And it is a sad commentary that so many fishery-based economies are struggling with dramatically lower harvests and incomes.

Despite knowledge of the economic, social, and environmental costs of open-access fisheries, remedies have been difficult to achieve. Various regulatory approaches have been adopted, including restrictive fishing seasons, rules on acceptable sizes and maturity of landed fish, and limits on the technology and equipment that can be used. None of these regulations, however, has been very successful. Fishers have resisted them, and regulators have modified them, but the results have not improved. The main problem is one of incentives. The regulations have not made fishers part of the solution. They have not made fishers the residual claimants to the value of a well-managed fishery. Property rights, like those assigned by ITQs, go a long way towards making fishers the 'owners' of the resource. Under ITQs, each fisher has a share of the total allowable catch (catch or output quotas) or of the total allowable fishing time (effort or input quotas). ITQs may be traded, depending on the nature of the system. Especially with catch quotas, fishers have incentives to protect the stock of fish since they have an annual claim on a portion of the harvest.

Despite the attractiveness of ITQs, Professor Gissurarson shows that their adoption has been slow and controversial in some fisheries. ITQs, as with all property rights, are political institutions. And various constituencies are affected by the adoption of quota systems. Unless parties can perceive that they will be made better off by any new arrangement, they will oppose it. The political process includes the bargaining and exchanges that are necessary to forge agreement. Where the parties are more homogeneous with respect to objectives, information, size, and costs, the more likely it will be that an agreement can be reached on property rights (Libecap, 1989). In contrast, where parties are more heterogeneous, agreements will be more difficult. Parties will seek quota arrangements that make them better off. Accordingly, some parties will seek effort quotas if they believe that they are more productive fishers than are their competitors, whereas others may seek catch quotas. The basis for quotas, whether they should be assigned according to historical catch or allocated uniformly, also will be in dispute. Additionally, conflicts may arise as to whether or not quotas should be freely transferable and accumulated by a small number of fishers. If effective, the adoption of ITQs should result in larger stocks, greater harvests and increased fishery-based wealth. Holders of ITQs should benefit, but this situation often brings distributional pressures to tax and redistribute wealth according to the notion that the fishery is a public resource. The imposition of taxes, however, dilutes the favourable incentive effects of well-defined property rights.

In this study, Hannes Gissurarson identifies each of these factors. He describes the comparatively later introduction of ITQs in the cod fishery relative to the herring fishery. He argues that the pelagic fishers were more homogeneous than were those in the demersal fisheries. In the herring fishery vessels were similar and had recent information about a collapse in the fishery, while in the cod fishery, there were important differences between fishing regions. Northwestern Icelandic fishers preferred effort quotas and the more distant southeastern fishers preferred catch quotas. It took time for catch quotas to be adopted, and they gradually emerged as the cod fishery moved from effort ITQs to a mixed catch/effort system to catch ITQs. The politics of this process have been heated. Small boats have been exempted from regulations, the concentration of quotas has been restricted, and taxes have been proposed. Further, the nature of the property right to be granted to ITQ holders has been challenged, and the court system has been brought in to adjudicate conflicting claims.

Douglass North (1990) emphasized the complexities of institutional change, even when there were large social benefits at stake. He argued that distributional concerns could block the introduction of more efficient property rights arrangements. This study by Hannes Gissurarson not only illustrates the complexities of institutional change, but it highlights the key factors involved. As such, it adds valuable empirical detail to our understanding of institutions and politics, and their implications for economic behavior.

Gary D. Libecap
University of Arizona and
National Bureau of Economic Research

July 2000

Cheung, Steven N.S. 1970, 'The Structure of a Contract and the Theory of a Non-Exclusive Resource,' *Journal of Law and Economics*, 13: 49-70.
Gordon, H. Scott 1954, 'The Economic Theory of a Common Property Resource: The Fishery,' *Journal of Political Economy*, 62: 124-42.
Hardin, Garrett 1968, 'The Tragedy of the Commons,' *Science* 162: 1243-8.
Libecap, Gary D. 1989, *Contracting for Property Rights*, New York: Cambridge University Press.
North, Douglass C. 1990 *Institutions, Institutional Change, and Economic Performance*, New York: Cambridge University Press.
Scott, Anthony 1955, 'The Fishery: The Objectives of Sole Ownership,' *Journal of Political Economy*, 63: 116-24.

The Author

Hannes H. Gissurarson received his B.A. and M.A. in History and Philosophy from the University of Iceland and a D.Phil. in Politics from Oxford University where he was the R.G. Collingwood Scholar at Pembroke College, 1984-5. In 1980, he first publicly suggested the development of private property rights in the Icelandic fisheries, in the form of individual transferable quotas, publishing a book in Icelandic on the subject in 1990. Professor of Politics at the University of Iceland since 1988, Gissurarson has been Visiting Scholar at the Hoover Institution, Stanford University, Visiting Professor at Libera Universita Internazionale degli Studi Sociale in Rome, Fellow at the International Centre for Economic Research in Turin, and Visiting Fulbright Scholar at the Department of Economics, University of California at Los Angeles. Professor Gissurarson is a Member of the Board of Directors of the Mont Pèlerin Society.

Introduction

According to the environmentalist group Greenpeace, commercial fishing fleets are exceeding the ocean's ecological limits. 'Instead of coming to grips with the need for dramatic cuts, nations argue over who will get how much of what remains of dwindling fish stocks. Meanwhile, the financial captains of the global fishing industry plough full steam ahead on their unsustainable, competitive rush to vacuum the oceans and turn fish into cash' (Greenpeace, 1997). Greenpeace asserts that modern technology is to blame. Here it will be argued, on the contrary, that modern technology has facilitated not only fishing and therefore overfishing, but also the management of the fisheries, or rather their self-management. By lowering transaction costs—costs of identifying harmful effects of economic activities, solving them in market transactions, implementing and enforcing the solutions, and so on—modern technology has made feasible the development of property rights to certain marine resources, in particular fish stocks.

Under a certain set of rules, therefore, individual owners of fishing capital can in market transactions further their private interests at the same time as they work for the public interest. A 'competitive rush' to harvest fish can, under certain circumstances, be not only sustainable, but also profitable. More than that: it can lead to the conservation and even the organised growth and improvement of fish stocks. A practical example, examined in this paper, is the way in which the Icelanders have coped with overfishing. They have developed a comprehensive system of individual transferable quotas, ITQs, in all commercially valuable fish stocks in their territorial waters, enabling them to 'turn fish into cash' without, at the same time, having to 'vacuum the oceans'.

Chapter 1 describes how the ITQ system arose in Iceland in response to declining fish stocks and decreasing catches in Icelandic waters in the early 1980s. It should be stressed, however, that the purpose of an efficient system of fishing is the maximisation not of catches, but of profits. The real fisheries problem is that under non-exclusive access to fishing grounds, fishing firms harm one another by their harvesting, in the form of over-capitalisation and excessive fishing effort. Chapter 2 describes how the Icelandic ITQ system works; how the total allowable catch, TAC, for each fish stock is set; how ITQs were initially allocated and what restrictions apply to their transfers; how the ITQ system is administered and enforced by government; and how the problem of migratory fish is solved.

Chapter 3 discusses the performance of the ITQ system in different types of fisheries found in the Icelandic waters, in the pelagic, demersal, and some small fisheries. Moreover, it discusses the impact of the ITQ system on Iceland's regional development and on the structure of the fisheries sector, for example the relative size of individual fishing firms and the concentration of quotas. It also identifies remaining problems of the ITQ system, especially highgrading and the uncertain legal status of ITQs. Chapter 4 discusses current controversies in Iceland on the ITQ system, on the one hand about the initial allocation of ITQs in the demersal fisheries and on the other hand about the distribution of the rent being captured by fishing firms, previously dissipated. The main conclusion of this paper can be briefly stated: Iceland's ITQ system, while definitely not perfect, and still somewhat controversial, works reasonably well and may be a model for other countries.

1. The Evolution of the ITQ System

While Iceland is a country poor in natural resources, the fishing grounds in Icelandic waters are some of the most fertile in the world. The Icelanders are therefore dependent on the fisheries for their recent affluence, with marine products providing more than 70% of total commodity exports. Demersal fish species, accounting for about 75% of the total value of marine products, include first and foremost cod, but also redfish, haddock, saithe, halibut, plaice and some less important species. Relatively territorial in nature, cod and other demersal species of fish are found in feeding grounds near the bottom of the shallow continental shelf around Iceland (therefore they are often called groundfish). On the other hand, herring and capelin are pelagic species: they are non-territorial or migratory fish, roaming in large schools over wide areas of the sea, usually near its surface. In addition to the demersal and pelagic fisheries, there are the small, but productive, scallop, nephrops (Norwegian lobster) and shrimp fisheries: those species are mostly harvested inshore, in clearly identifiable fishing grounds, although some deep-sea shrimp is also found.

When it finally began to be understood in the 20th century that fishing grounds were not inexhaustible resources, any attempt to limit the access to those in the Icelandic waters was made difficult by the fact that no single country had clear jurisdiction over them. Indeed, in the 1952-76 period Iceland fought four 'Cod Wars' with the United Kingdom for control over those fishing grounds, unilaterally extending Iceland's Exclusive Economic Zone, EEZ, first to 4 nautical miles, then to 12 miles, then to 50 miles, and finally to 200 miles. Iceland's two main arguments were that those extensions of the EEZ made the necessary conservation of fish stocks possible and that the Icelanders, unlike other nations in the North Atlantic Ocean, were totally dependent on fishing. When the United Kingdom recognised Iceland's 200 miles EEZ, shown in Figure 1, and the last British trawler sailed out of Iceland's territorial waters on December 1st, 1976, the legal prerequisites for the management of the Icelandic fisheries finally were in place—and not too soon, as subsequent events showed.

Figure 1 – The Icelandic EEZ

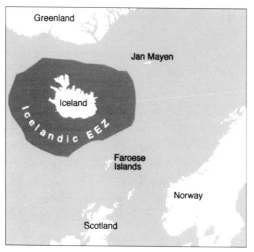

Effort Quotas, 1977-83

It has already been noted that the Icelandic demersal and pelagic fisheries were quite different in nature. But because of this difference, the pelagic and demersal fishing fleets were also different in composition. Boats of a similar (medium) size harvested most of the pelagic fish, herring and capelin, whereas the demersal fishing fleet was heterogeneous, comprising large freezer trawlers, mid-size multi-purpose vessels as well as small boats, even some undecked rowboats. The relative importance of the two kinds of fisheries also varied by regions. Since the most fertile demersal fishing grounds lay in the northwestern part of Iceland's EEZ, fishing vessels from the Northwest, that is from the Western Fjords, were in a better position to harvest fish there than vessels from other regions. Hence, fishing villages in the Western Fjords relied mostly on harvesting cod and other demersal species of fish.

The pelagic fisheries, on the other hand, were non-territorial, herring and capelin being chased all over the Icelandic waters and even outside them. They were more important to the fishing villages in the East than to those in the Western Fjords. Another fact undoubtedly had some effect on the evolution of the ITQ system. In the late 1960s, the Icelanders had had a first-hand experience of the dire consequences of overfishing. After a 'herring boom' of the early 1960s, with annual catches of herring approaching 600,000 metric tonnes (MT), the herring stock collapsed in 1967-8, so that a moratorium was imposed on the herring fishery in 1972, with harvesting resuming on a small scale in 1975. Soon after the extension of the EEZ to 200 miles, a special Fisheries Act was passed by Parliament, in 1976, giving the Minister of Fisheries wide powers to restrict access to the fishing grounds in Icelandic waters, while it was not clearly specified in which ways he should do so.

In 1976 the Icelandic Marine Research Institute, MRI, warned that the cod stock was threatened by overfishing. Fish mortality was alarmingly high, and the spawning stock was weak. The MRI recommended a total allowable catch in cod of 230,000 MT for that year, while the actual total catch turned out to be 350,000 MT. Vessel owners in the demersal fisheries now were also beginning to realise that the cod stock, the mainstay of the Icelandic economy, accounting for about 35% of the total value of marine products, was in danger of collapse similar to that of the herring stock a decade earlier, still fresh in their memory. Obviously, access to the demersal fishing grounds had to be restricted. There was much discussion whether such restrictions should be in terms of effort or of catch.

Finally it was decided to restrict effort, that is, allowable fishing time, rather than vessel catch. In 1977, effort quotas in the demersal fisheries were introduced. While entry remained more or less free, and there were no restrictions on the catch of each fishing vessel, allowable fishing days were to be reduced until the desired result in terms of total allowable demersal catch had been reached. The Minister of Fisheries in 1974-8 came from the Western Fjords, where support for effort quotas was strongest. Because fishing villages in the Western Fjords were closest to the most fertile cod grounds, vessel owners there thought that they would always be at an advantage in competition in terms of unlimited harvesting during a limited period of time. However, it soon became clear that effort quotas were wasteful. This system induced owners of fishing vessels to start a 'Derby', that is a competitive rush to harvest as much fish as possible during allowable fishing days. The objective became the largest possible catch in the shortest possible time, regardless of cost. Since entry remained almost free, this meant not only that existing fishing capacity was not utilised economically, but also that there was an incentive to add to it. The already too large fishing fleet became still larger, while the number of allowable fishing days had to be reduced almost every year. For deep-sea trawlers, for example, the number of fishing days went down from 323 in 1977 to 215 in 1981. Moreover, total annual actual catches consistently, and by far exceeded the total annual allowable catches recommended by the MRI.

The Introduction of Vessel Catch Quotas, 1983-4

In Iceland, 1978-83 were years of weak governments, political upheavals and uncertainties. But in the summer of 1983 a strong coalition government of the Independence Party (Iceland's conservative party, with 35-40% of the votes) and the Progressive Party (with rural roots and about 20% of the votes) was formed. The new Minister of Fisheries, Halldor Asgrimsson, who came from the East region, was to remain in office for the next eight years. He worked closely with the powerful Association of Fishing Vessel Owners whose leader, Kristjan Ragnarsson, was becoming convinced, with many of his members, that effort quotas did not work. In late 1983, the MRI found that the cod stock was still weakening. The spawning stock was at an all-time low, estimated at only 200,000 MT; and fish mortality was very high. Even if the total actual catch of cod had gone down from 461,000 MT in 1981 to 294,000 MT in 1983, it exceeded that recommended by the MRI by 100,000 MT. It was also becoming ever clearer that there was massive over-investment in the fisheries. This is shown in Figure 2: in 1945-83, fishing capital increased by well over 1200%, while real catch values only increased by 300%. Thus, the growth of fishing capital exceeded the increase in catch values by a factor of more than four.

At the same time as vessel owners in the demersal fisheries could observe massive over-investment there, a sharp reduction in the number of allowable fishing days, and a clear decline in the cod stock, they witnessed the relative success of vessel catch quotas in the pelagic fisheries. After the herring moratorium of 1972-5, it had been decided to set an annual total allowable catch, TAC, of herring over each year's fishing season, and to divide this TAC equally between the herring boats in operation. This was a simple and non-controversial rule of initial allocation since the herring boats were all of roughly equal size and with a similar catch history. In 1979, those vessel catch quotas had been, at the initiative of the herring boat owners, made transferable: they had become ITQs. Arguably, this was one of the first ITQ systems in world fisheries. Similarly, in the capelin fishery, vessel catch quotas had been introduced in 1980, at the initiative of the capelin boat owners, to be made transferable in 1986. In both of those pelagic fisheries, such vessel catch quotas had had the effect to reduce boats at the same time as catch increased.

Figure 2
Fishing Capital and Catch Values 1945-1997
(index 1960=100). Source: National Economic Institute

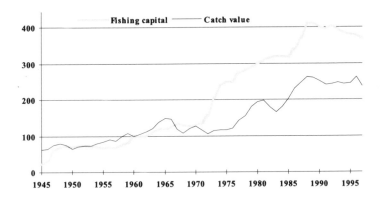

The most vocal support for the introduction of vessel catch quotas in the demersal fisheries came from the East, whereas vessel owners in the Western Fjords continued to favour effort quotas. In 1983 the supporters of vessel catch quotas finally gained the upper hand in the Association of Fishing Vessel Owners, and at the annual meeting of the Icelandic Fisheries Association—a broad collection of interest groups in the fisheries—in December 1983, a resolution was passed calling on the Minister of Fisheries to experiment with vessel catch quotas in the demersal fisheries, especially in the all-important cod fishery. The Minister of Fisheries promptly proposed an amendment to the original Fisheries Act of 1976, giving him discretionary power to issue individual quotas for each vessel employed in the demersal fisheries for the year 1984. After much, and heated, discussion, the Icelandic Parliament passed the amendment at the end of December 1983, in the Upper House with a bare majority of one vote. Consequently, the Minister of Fisheries set a TAC for each demersal species of fish for the year 1984 and issued shares in those TACs to each and every fishing vessel. The catch vessel quotas were allocated on the basis of catch history over the preceding three years, from November 1st 1981 to October 1st 1983, with exceptions to correct for certain situations, for instance if a vessel had entered the demersal fisheries during those three years or if it had been under repair for part of this period.

New vessels could choose between the new kinds of quotas and the old effort quotas (restrictions in terms of allowable fishing days). The new vessel catch quotas were partly transferable. Transfers of quotas between vessels under the same ownership or vessels from the same port were allowed, but transfers between vessels from different ports were only allowed if they were exchanges (such as a quota in redfish for a quota in cod), otherwise such transfers had to be approved by the Minister of Fisheries. Small boats, under 10 Gross Registered Tonnes (GRT), were exempt from the quota system; they could harvest fish at will until they reached a total quota set for this type of vessel.

A Mixed System, 1985-90

It is easy to see why vessel catch quotas were initially differently allocated in the demersal and pelagic fisheries. While the herring and capelin boats were of roughly the same size, making an equal initial allocation of vessel catch quotas between them fairly straightforward,[1] there were vast differences between individual

---

1   In the capelin fishery, for complicated historical reasons, two-thirds of the vessel catch quotas initially were allocated equally, and one-third on the basis of vessel hold capacity.

vessels in the demersal fisheries, so the more complicated rule of catch history over the preceding three years had to be adopted, with small boats even exempted altogether from the system. At the end of 1984, when the experience of the previous twelve months under a system of vessel catch quotas was reviewed, it was generally accepted that these kinds of quotas had been much more effective in halting overfishing than effort quotas. It was therefore decided to extend the amendment to the Fisheries Act of 1976 for one more year, allowing the Minister of Fisheries to issue vessel catch quotas for 1985. The opposition to vessel catch quotas from the Western Fjords remained strong, however, so, as a compromise, vessel owners were now allowed to choose between vessel catch quotas and effort quotas. This meant that a typical vessel owner could either hold on to the share of the TAC which had been issued to him at the end of 1983, and harvest fish up to the limit set by that share; or he could give up his vessel catch quota and try instead to harvest as much as he could in the allowable fishing days, whose number was set by the Minister of Fisheries on the basis of predictions about their contribution to the TAC.

This mixed system of vessel catch quotas and effort quotas was in effect for the next six years, until the end of 1990. At the end of 1985, when the experience of the previous two years was reviewed, it was decided to write the system into a special law, the Fisheries Management Act, instead of passing an amendment to the Fisheries Act of 1976, as had been done in 1983 and 1984. It was also decided to issue the vessel catch quotas for two years, 1986 and 1987, instead of for one year. Earlier restrictions on access to certain fishing areas (for example, spawning grounds) and on allowable fishing gear (for example, mesh size) also continued to apply; and in addition to catch quotas, owners of fishing vessels had to hold special fishing permits which were in effect restricted to those who had operated vessels in the first years after the introduction of quotas.

When the Fisheries Management Act came up for review in the Icelandic Parliament at the end of 1987, difficult negotiations began, extending into the first weeks of 1988. The Icelandic Social Democrats (with about 15% of the votes), in a rather weak coalition government with the Independence Party and the Progressive Party since 1987, now insisted on inserting a declaration into the Act to the effect that the fish stocks were 'the common property' of the Icelandic nation. It was also decided in 1988 to extend the duration of the vessel catch quotas from two to three years, from 1988 to the end of 1990, and to make an extensive review of the system in 1990.

Another important change in the 1988 Act was that it now applied not only to the demersal fisheries. The vessel catch quotas developed in the herring and capelin fisheries from 1975 have already been briefly described. But the nephrops, shrimp and scallop fisheries were quite unlike both the demersal and the pelagic fisheries. They were confined to certain well-defined inshore fishing grounds and from their beginning in the 1960s and 1970s they were subject to local restrictions on entry. In 1973, a TAC in nephrops was first set and vessel catch quotas issued to vessels. A year later, two of the seven inshore shrimp grounds were already subject to vessel catch quotas. In 1975, vessel catch quotas were issued in the inshore shrimp and scallop fisheries. Since boats operating in the nephrops, shrimp and scallop fisheries were all of roughly similar size, vessel catch quotas were initially allocated equally. Another important change in the 1988 Fisheries Management Act was that it was made difficult or even impossible for vessels which had chosen to operate on effort quotas to increase their share in the TAC. A further problem addressed in the 1988 Fisheries Management Act was that of the great increase in the number of small boats, under 10 GRT, which had taken place since 1983-4, in response to their exemption from limits on entry (most of the new boats being just under 10 GRT in volume). It was now decided to subject boats between 6 and 10 GRT to fishing permits and to issue no new permits to new boats of this size, unless they replaced old ones.

A Comprehensive System of ITQs, 1990

When the Fisheries Management Act was revised in the spring of 1990, it was the first time this was done without the threat of an immediate collapse of any fish stock. The discussion therefore centred on the main objectives of fisheries management. Most of those concerned recognised that vessel catch quotas had turned out to be superior to effort quotas. A vessel owner who received a given share in the TAC, in the form of ITQs, could concentrate on harvesting this share in the most efficient way over each season; if he was successful in doing this, he would have an incentive to buy additional quotas from other less successful vessel owners.

In a book which I published on this issue in the Spring of 1990, while the Icelandic Parliament was discussing the revision of the Fisheries Management Act, I argued that the system of ITQs was reasonably efficient and that it should be developed as far as possible into a system of private property rights (Gissurarson, 1990).[2] The two Icelandic specialists in fisheries economics, Professor Ragnar Arnason of the University of Iceland and Professor Rognvaldur Hannesson of the Norwegian Business School in Bergen, also argued, in reports to the Parliament, that the ITQs should be maintained, but that limits on their transferability and duration should be abolished. Perhaps most importantly, the Association of Fishing Vessel Owners, under the forceful leadership of Kristjan Ragnarsson, also supported ITQs and argued for their increased transferability. The opposition to ITQs was strong, however. First, vessel owners in the Western Fjords still preferred effort quotas. Secondly, there were those who wanted small boats to remain exempt from any quotas, often for romantic reasons. In the third group which had been slowly forming over the preceding few years, there were those who opposed what they perceived to be trends towards the development of private property rights in the fisheries. Some members of this third group wanted to impose a special tax on the fisheries

---

2   In September 1980, I had first argued for the development of private property rights in the fisheries, at a conference on 'Iceland in the Year 2000', organised by Iceland's Management Society. In April 1983, almost a year before individual quotas were first introduced in the demersal fisheries, I argued for recognising the traditional and existing fishing rights as property rights and making them marketable. 'This would mean that the initial allocation of property rights would be the share in the catch. . . . The market is not constructed. It is developed out of existing institutions. It simply consists in handing over responsibility to the fishermen themselves, in directing their self-interest to the preservation and, it is to be hoped, to the multiplication of the stock' (Gissurarson, 1983).

aimed at expropriating the economic rent which holders of quotas would derive from the exclusive access to and utilisation of a scarce resource (Jonsson, 1975); others called on government to take the ITQs from vessel owners and to rent them back to them, in special auctions (Gylfason, 1990).

In 1990, the Icelandic Parliament passed a new Fisheries Management Act. It took effect in the beginning of January, 1991, whereas the fishing season was redefined from September 1st each year to August 31st next year.[3] The three important changes in the system were that effort quotas in the demersal fisheries were abolished, their holders receiving vessel catch quotas instead, that the quotas were issued for an indefinite period of time and that they became fully transferable. In essence, a comprehensive system of individual transferable quotas, ITQs, now replaced a mixed system of vessel catch quotas and effort quotas. By the 1990 Fisheries Management Act fishing vessels between 6 and 10 MT were also integrated into the ITQ system, receiving share quotas in place of the effort restrictions under which they had previously operated.

Opposition to the ITQ system remained strong, however, and in the 1990 Fisheries Management Act two concessions were made to it. First, boats under 6 GRT remained exempt from the system and subject, for a limited adjustment time, to effort restrictions (a given number of fishing days). Secondly, at the insistence of the Social Democrats, a paragraph was inserted into the Fisheries Management Act to the effect that no assignment of ITQs by this law could constitute any permanent property rights to such quotas or become the ground for compensation if the quotas were taken from their holders. While neither of these concessions seemed important at the time, they both turned out to be unfortunate. The

---

3 This was done in order to direct harvesting of fish away from the summer months, when quality suffers more quickly and regular factory workers are on vacation. There are a few exceptions. In 1999-2000, for example, the fishing season for Icelandic herring is set from September 1st 1999 to May 1st 2000 and for inshore shrimp it is October 1st 1999 to May 1st 2000. Harvesting of herring from the Atlanto-Scandian stock, of oceanic redfish in the Irminger Sea and of deep-sea shrimp on the Flemish Cap is also subject to special regulations by international agreements.

exemption of small boats from the ITQ system created a loophole in the 'fence' erected around the Icelandic fishing grounds; and the paragraph in the 1990 Fisheries Management Act about the impossibility of permanent property rights in ITQs left the legal status of quotas unclear.

Further Developments in the ITQ System, 1990-2000

When the new and comprehensive Fisheries Management Act was passed in 1990, it was stipulated that it should be revised after three years. In 1991, a new and strong coalition government of the Independence Party and the Social Democrats was formed, with former Prime Minister Thorsteinn Palsson replacing Halldor Asgrimsson as Minister of Fisheries. Palsson was to remain Minister of Fisheries for the next eight years, contributing, like his predecessor, much to the development of the ITQ system. In 1993, the two government parties worked out a compromise about the vocal demands, supported by the Social Democrats, for some form of special taxation of quotas. The compromise was that a small 'service fee' was imposed on quota holders, the revenue from which was used to facilitate the reduction of the fishing fleet. In the same year, a public commission on fisheries management came to the conclusion in a report to the government that the ITQ system worked quite well but that some minor changes would make it more efficient. The commission recommended the integration of small boats, under 6 MT, into the system and making the ITQs transferable not only between vessels but also to fish processing plants. It also recommended that certain privileges of boats using longline in winter should be abolished and that holders of ITQs should not be allowed to depreciate quotas that they had bought, since fish stocks were renewable natural resources. The Association of Fishing Vessel Owners opposed the idea that quotas should be transferable to others than vessel owners, and this recommendation was not accepted by the Icelandic Parliament. The commission's other recommendations were mostly accepted, after much deliberation. In 1996 the privileges of boats using longline in winter were abolished, while those who had enjoyed those privileges received additional ITQs in compensation. Since 1998, holders of ITQs have not been allowed to depreciate quotas that they have bought.

The politically most difficult change has been the integration of boats under 6 GRT into the system. Mainly living in fishing villages in the countryside, with disproportionate representation in the Parliament, the owners of small boats form a strong interest group in Iceland. They managed to extend their adjustment period from 1994 to 1996 when they were allowed to choose between receiving vessel quotas, thus entering the ITQ system, or to remain subject to effort quotas (which became less and less attractive, as the number of allowable fishing days was reduced year-by-year). Another compromise was reached by government and owners of small boats in 1997, further facilitating their integration into the ITQ system. However, some small boats (about one-third of the total fleet of about 1,100 small boats) still remain outside the ITQ system.

Some further minor additions and amendments have been made to the 1990 Fisheries Management Acts. In 1997, two fish stocks harvested by international agreements outside Iceland's EEZ were integrated into the ITQ system: oceanic redfish in the Irminger Sea, southwest of Iceland's territorial waters, and deep-sea shrimp, in the so-called Flemish Cap east of Canadian territorial waters. Since 1998, two new rules have been applied to discourage speculation in quotas. One rule is that while a vessel may transfer some of her quota between fishing seasons, she will forfeit all her quota if she catches less than 50% of her total quota in two subsequent years. The other new rule is that within each year, the net transfer of quota (that is, the annual catch entitlement, not the permanent share of the TAC) from any vessel must not exceed 50%.

Another rule has been adopted to try to counter the possible concentration of quotas. It is that no fishing firm may control more than a 10% of the ITQs in cod and haddock and more than 20% of the ITQs in saithe, redfish, Greenland halibut, herring, deep-sea shrimp and capelin. In 1998, after bitter complaints from fishermen's unions that the crew of fishing vessels were forced to participate in quota purchases (that is, to have the cost of renting quota deducted from the total net revenue shared at the end of the fishing season by the vessel owner, captain and crew), it was decided to establish a special Quota Exchange. It is an institution for recording all quota transactions, to ensure that they are transparent and public. All quota transfers have to take place through the Quota Exchange except transfers from one vessel to another owned by the same fishing firm, or exchanges of quotas of the same value (but in different species of fish), or transfers that are deemed by the Minister of Fisheries not to have a market value.

Legal Decisions on ITQs

The ITQ system has further evolved in a series of decisions by the Icelandic courts and other authorities on the legal status of ITQs. One problem arises from the fact that holders of ITQs can either sell their right to harvest a given share in the TAC (their TAC-shares), or they can rent it over a season (their annual catch entitlement, the multiple of the TAC and the TAC-share). How should the incomes and outlays generated by such transfers be taxed? In 1993, the Supreme Court decided that the transfer of a permanent TAC-share should be taxed as transfer of property, but that the transfer of the right to harvest a given amount over one season (the annual catch entitlement) should be taxed as income for the seller and cost for the buyer. Another problem was caused because the Icelandic Parliament has not been ready to recognise the use of quotas as direct collaterals, despite proposals to that effect from the Minister of Fisheries. Predictably, banks and other lending institutions have circumvented this problem by writing into contracts with vessel owners that quotas issued to vessels used as collaterals cannot be transferred from those vessels without the lenders' consent. In 1996, a district judge decided that ITQs could not be used as such indirect collaterals, since the fish stocks were the declared common property of the Icelandic nation. The Supreme Court, in two decisions in 1999, did however recognise ITQs as indirect collaterals of the fishing vessels to which they were issued. It has also been decided, although not in court cases, that inheritance tax has to be paid of the (market value) of ITQs and that they should also be treated as property in the case of divorce.

The aforementioned cases were all about clarifying the legal status of the ITQs, for purposes of taxation and financial transactions. But opponents of the ITQ system have referred two matters of principle to the courts. In late 1998, the Supreme Court decided that requiring people who wanted to harvest fish in the Icelandic waters to hold not only ITQs but also special fishing permits (which were non-transferable and in effect confined to (owners of) fishing vessels operating in the first years of the ITQ system, in 1984-8, or to their replacements) was indeed unconstitutional. According to the court, to restrict entry into the fisheries in this way to a mostly closed group of people who happened to operate fishing vessels over a given period of time violated the two constitutional principles of economic freedom and equal treatment under the Law. While the special fishing permits were not an integral part of the ITQ system (and only imposed as a short-term measure to try to control the enlargement of the fishing fleet), its opponents rejoiced at this decision. The government promptly changed the law, so now fishing permits are not confined to (owners of) vessels in operation in 1984-8.

The other case was much more important because it was about the ITQs themselves. In early 2000, a district judge (in the Western Fjords) decided that the initial allocation of ITQs in the demersal fisheries, on the basis of catch history in 1981-3, had violated the constitutional principles of economic freedom and equal treatment before the Law. According to the judge, this method of allocation unfairly discriminated between the group of quota recipients and other Icelanders. In the spring of 2000 the Supreme Court reversed this decision. It decided that the initial allocation of ITQs, on the basis of catch history, had not included any arbitrary or unconstitutional discrimination against those who did not receive such ITQs. In the initial allocation, it was, the Supreme Court stated, quite fair and relevant to treat differently those who had a vested interest in continuing to harvest fish in the Icelandic waters, and all the others who had no such clear interest. Moreover, unlike the fishing permits, ITQs were transferable so they were not confined to any narrow group of people in the same way as the fishing permits had been. In the same decision, the Supreme Court stated that the general restriction of access to the Icelandic waters to holders of ITQs did not seem to violate the constitutional principle of economic freedom since this restriction had clearly been necessary in the face of collapsing fish stocks and unprofitable fishing firms.

Concluding Remarks

The evolution of the Icelandic ITQ system was a process of gradual discovery and difficult bargaining. Initially, politicians, marine biologists and vessel owners were mainly concerned about the conservation of fish stocks. It was only later that they came to realise the economic problem of unlimited access to a limited resource, the 'tragedy of the commons' (Hardin, 1968). From an economic point of view overfishing is similar to pollution. Where access to a fishing ground is free, the cost of adding one more vessel (or another unit of fishing capital) to the fishing fleet on the ground is not borne solely by the vessel owner. His activity has harmful effects on others. The consequences are over-capitalisation and excessive fishing effort. The fishing fleet is much larger than would be most efficient. As an illustration, sixteen boats may be harvesting a lesser catch than that which eight boats could easily harvest.

There is one big difference, however, between pollution and overfishing. Pollution is visible, whereas the economic costs that owners of fishing capital impose on one another are invisible. Those costs can be, and have been, demonstrated by economists (Gordon, 1954; Scott, 1955), but vessel owners usually come to realise the problem when it is too late—when fishing is exceeding not only the level of highest return on outlays, but also the maximum sustainable yield. Memories of the collapse of herring in the late 1960s may however have facilitated the acceptance by Icelandic vessel owners of what was in effect the enclosure of fishing grounds. Desperation lessens transaction costs (Libecap, 1989).

Another factor lessening transaction costs is homogeneity. Because Iceland's pelagic fisheries were relatively homogeneous, with similar vessels, the introduction of vessel catch quotas and later ITQs was relatively easy. The bargaining process was much more difficult in the heterogeneous demersal fisheries. Owners of small boats, some of them working part-time, did not think, for example, that they had much in common with owners of large freezer trawlers. Indeed, as we have seen, some small boats are still outside the ITQ system. And vessel owners in villages close to the most fertile fishing grounds also thought that they had different interests from other vessel owners, and their strong opposition delayed the introduction of a comprehensive ITQ system for many years.

The main lesson to be learned from this process is that the introduction of ITQs in a fishery, however necessary it may seem to politicians, marine biologists and economists, is by no means a simple task. There are all kinds of interests which may oppose it. A commons like the fish stocks in Icelandic waters will only be enclosed if the private interests of those utilising the commons are made to coincide with the public interest. It was probably crucial for the evolution of the Icelandic ITQ system that the Association of Fishing Vessel Owners repeatedly took the initiative in the process, and that government worked closely with it (Jonsson, 1990), although it inevitably led critics to say that government was in the thrall of the Association of Fishing Vessel Owners. But a cart without a horse to drive it, is of little use.

The really important question is: 'Who Cares Whether the Commons is Privatised?' (Buchanan, 1997). It is difficult to see, for example, how vessel owners in the Icelandic demersal fisheries would have agreed to any other initial allocation of quotas in late 1983 than that which was based on catch history. This was the only way for them to continue utilising the fish stocks without much disruption. In this way they could maintain the value of their investments and human capital whereas it would have become almost worthless if government had auctioned off individual quotas to the highest bidders, as some economists proposed.

In essence, the problem in the Icelandic fisheries was the same as in all fisheries utilising modern technology, and operating under free access to fishing grounds: It was, to return to our illustration, that sixteen boats were harvesting even less than that which eight boats could easily harvest. The task therefore was to reduce the number of boats from sixteen to eight. In theory, this could be accomplished by outbidding the owners of the eight excessive boats, by taxation or in an auction of quotas. But in practice, this would have been difficult, if not impossible. In the Icelandic case, what was done was to assign transferable quotas sufficient for the profitable operation of eight boats, to the owners of sixteen boats. Over time, the eight boat owners who wanted to continue harvesting fish would have a great incentive to buy quotas from their eight colleagues who for one reason or another wanted to leave the fishery. Thus, people were not outbid; they were bought out.

Table 1
Main Stages in the Evolution
of the Icelandic ITQ System

1975 Individual quotas in herring fishery

1979 Quotas in herring fishery transferable

1980 Individual quotas in capelin fishery

1983 Vessel owners recommend individual quotas in demersal fisheries

1984 Individual (mostly) transferable quotas in demersal fisheries. Issued for a year

1985 Effort quota option in demersal fisheries. ITQs issued for a year

1986 Individual quotas in capelin fishery transferable. ITQs issued for two years (1986-7)

1988 Individual transferable quotas in all fisheries. Effort quota option retained. ITQs issued for three years (1988-90)

1990 Fisheries Management Act to apply from 1 January 1991

1991 Comprehensive system of transferable share quotas in all fisheries for all vessels over 6 GRT. Effort quota option removed

1993 Supreme Court decides ITQs be taxed as property

1996 Exemptions of vessels using longline in winter abolished; boats under 6 GRT mostly integrated into ITQ system

1997 Harvesting outside Iceland's EEZ mostly made subject to the ITQ system

1998 Quota Exchange; legal restrictions on speculation in and concentration of ITQs

2000 Supreme Court upholds initial allocation of ITQs on basis of catch history

2. The Nature of the ITQ System

Economists analysing the 'tragedy of the commons'—the over-utilisation of non-exclusive natural resources—generally agree that the tragedy is caused by the absence of private property rights to those resources. In the costly race to extract value from such resources, whether they are plots of land, oilfields, mines, or fish stocks, the rent which could be derived from them is dissipated. 'The business of everybody is the business of nobody.' It was only with the enclosure of land, for example, that the problem of overgrazing was solved, and cultivation replaced simple extraction. The EEZs which fishing nations have established in the 20th century may be regarded as important steps towards the enclosure of marine resources.

At first sight, however, private property rights in areas of the sea or in individual specimens of fish do not seem technologically feasible, at least not in deep-sea fisheries; such rights would require techniques of fencing or branding, either non-existent or difficult to develop. ITQs may however go far to solve the fisheries problem (Arnason, 1990), precisely because they have some characteristics of private property rights: they are exclusive which means that only those who hold them may harvest fish; they are individual so that the responsibility for their utilisation is clearly defined and lies with individuals; they are divisible which enables fishing firms freely to decide how much of them to hold at any given time; they are transferable which means that market forces are allowed to select the most efficient fishing firms; and they are permanent, making long-term planning possible.

ITQs are not too difficult to administer or enforce, either, although the political problem of their introduction and initial allocation should not be minimised. Therefore, it is not surprising that ITQs are increasingly being used in world fisheries. Between 5 and 10% of world total catches are presently harvested under some kinds of vessel catch quotas. Iceland and New Zealand are the only two countries to have developed a comprehensive ITQ system although ITQs are also widely used in the Netherlands, Australia and some other countries. Despite some weaknesses, the Icelandic ITQ system does not seem too different from the system described by economists as going far to solve the fisheries problem.

TACs

The two pillars of the Icelandic ITQ system are total allowable catches (TACs), and individual transferable quotas (ITQs). TACs are set annually by the Minister of Fisheries for each of the commercially valuable species of fish in Icelandic waters, on the basis of recommendations from the Marine Research Institute, (MRI). Economic considerations—receiving the maximum return on fishing capital—do not seem to play an important role in the setting of TACs although that may change in the future. In the first few years after the introduction of ITQs in the demersal fisheries, the Minister of Fisheries tended to set somewhat larger TACs than recommended by the MRI, mainly because as a politician he was concerned about adverse effects on the economy by sharp reductions in TACs, especially in the fishing villages scattered around Iceland's coastline. This has gradually changed, especially after 1991. In 1995, government even adopted a special rule about the annual TAC in cod: it is to be set at 25% of the fishable biomass, as estimated by the MRI. Thus, the TAC is determined in and by the annual stock assessment. By applying this rule, marine biologists estimate that the chances of stock collapse go down to less than 1%. In June 2000, as this paper was going to the printers, the government revised the rule in order to stabilise the setting of TACs in cod between years. It stipulated that the difference in TACs between years should not exceed 30,000 MT. The MRI had reported weak classes of cod for harvesting in 1999-2001, with an expected strengthening of the stock thereafter. Therefore the cod TAC was set at 220,000 MT for 2000-2001, compared with 203,000 MT under the old rule. Table 2 reproduces the recommendations in 1984-2000 by the MRI for the TAC in cod, the decision by the Minister of Fisheries, and the actual total catch.

Table 2
Recommended and Set TACs in Cod
and Total Actual Catches, 1984-2000
(In MT)

Year	Recommended TAC (MRI)	Allocated TAC (Ministry of Fisheries)	Actual Total Catch
1984	200,000	242,000	281,000
1985	200,000	263,000	323,000
1986	300,000	300,000	365,000
1987	300,000	330,000	390,000
1988	300,000	350,000	376,000
1989	300,000	325,000	354,000
1990	250,000	300,000	333,000
1991	240,000	245,000	245,000
1991-2	250,000	265,000	273,000
1992-3	190,000	205,000	240,000
1993-4	150,000	165,000	196,000
1994-5	130,000	155,000	164,000
1995-6	155,000	155,000	169,000
1996-7	186,000	186,000	201,000
1997-8	218,000	218,000	227,000
1998-9	250,000	250,000	N. A.
1999-2000	247,000	250,000	N. A.

Source: Marine Research Institute.

The sharp reductions in TACs of cod in 1994-6 are noteworthy. If the members of the Association of Fishing Vessel Owners had not by then begun to think of themselves as stakeholders in the cod fishery, it is doubtful that such sharp reductions could have been accomplished relatively peacefully in a country as heavily dependent on fishing as Iceland is. Table 3 reproduces the TACs of different species of fish, set by the Minister of Fisheries, for the fishing season 1999-2000.

Table 3
TACs in Different Species of Fish
for the Fishing Year 1999-2000
(In MT)

Stock	TAC Recommendation (MRI)	TAC Allocation (Ministry of Fisheries)
Demersal species		
Atlantic cod	247,000	250,000
Haddock	35,000	35,000
Saithe (Atlantic pollock)	25,000	30,000
Golden redfish (ocean perch)	35,000	35,000
Oceanic redfish (ocean perch)	25,000	25,000
Greenland halibut	10,000	10,000
Ocean catfish	13,000	13,000
Plaice	4,000	4,000
Witch	1,100	1,100
Dab	7,000	7,000
Lemon sole	1,400	1,400
Long rough dab	5,000	5,000
Other species		
Icelandic herring	100,000	100,000
Scallop (all areas)	9,800	9,800
Nephrops (Norway lobster)	1,200	1,200
Inshore shrimp	3,300	3,300
Deep-sea shrimp	20,000	20,000
Capelin	575,850	575,850

Source: Marine Research Institute.

Of the 1999-2000 TAC in cod, almost 35,000 MT were reserved for small boats fishing with handline and longline and some 6,500 MT for other purposes, chiefly to compensate for setbacks in other fisheries. A portion of the TACs in haddock, saithe and catfish was reserved in a similar way. It should be mentioned that 1999-2000 TACs for inshore and deep-sea shrimp were provisional, in line with the recommendations of the MRI and pending further research and stock assessment. The TAC in capelin was also provisional; it was Iceland's share in the total negotiated TAC in capelin (856,000 MT) in the Northeast Atlantic Ocean.

ITQs

ITQs constitute the other pillar of the Icelandic fisheries system. ITQs are shares in the TAC of a fish stock. They are issued to each vessel for an indefinite period of time, in the demersal fisheries initially, as described in Chapter 1, on the basis of catch history in 1981-3. The only vessels partly exempt from the system are boats under 6 MT whose owners have chosen to operate under effort restrictions (a given number of allowable fishing days). They harvest, however, a small proportion of the total demersal catch. The ITQs are transferable both annually and permanently. A legal distinction is therefore made between two kinds of transferable quotas issued to a vessel: her TAC-share, given in percentages, and her Annual Catch Entitlement, ACE, given in MT, where the ACE is a simple multiple of the TAC for the fishery, and the vessel's TAC-share. For example, if a deep-sea trawler initially received a 0.1% share of the TAC in cod, and if the TAC in the fishing season 1999-2000 is 250,000 MT, then the owner of that vessel may use it to harvest 250 MT of cod in the given year and expect to harvest 0.1% of the TACs set in coming years. His TAC- share is 0.1%, and his ACE in 1999-2000 is 250 MT.

He can do one of three things with his quota: 1) he can himself harvest 250 MT over the 1999-2000 season; 2) while keeping his TAC-share, he can sell his ACE, or a part of it, to the owner of another vessel, that is the right to harvest 250 MT, or a part of it, over the 1999-2000 season; 3) he can sell his TAC-share, that is the right to harvest 0.1% share in the TACs set now and in coming years.

Both the TAC-shares and the ACEs are perfectly divisible. The TAC-shares are also perfectly transferable. There are some restrictions on transfers of ACEs, however, with the objective of stabilising local employment. While ACEs can be freely transferred between vessels under the same ownership or within the same region, their transfers between vessels in different regions have to be approved by the Minister of Fisheries after a review by the regional fishermen's union and local authorities. Since few transfers are blocked, in practice the ACEs can be regarded as freely transferable. Over time most of the ITQs have indeed changed hands: In February 2000 only 19% of the quotas initially allocated in the demersal fisheries were still held by those who originally received them (Morgunbladid, 2000).

Since the Icelandic fisheries are mixed fisheries, vessels are bound to come up with different species of fish on the same fishing trips, haddock as well as cod or redfish, to name a few. The TAC-shares in different fish stocks therefore have to be interchangeable. But species of fish differ in value: 1 MT of cod is for example worth much more than 1 MT of capelin. Cod is therefore used as the common denominator of the system. The term 'cod equivalent' denotes the relative market value of different species of fish, set by a regulation every year. For each vessel having a quota for several species the total quota may be calculated in cod equivalents. Quota transfers between vessels are also often measured in cod equivalents. In the fishing season from September 1st 1998 to August 31st 1999, the cod equivalent values were, for example, as follows: cod 1.00, haddock 1.05, saithe 0.65, redfish 0.70, plaice 1.20, Greenland halibut 2.15, ocean catfish 0.85, witch 1.20, dab 0.65, long rough dab 0.60, capelin 0.08, herring 0.14, nephrops 8.55, shrimp 1.20 and scallops 0.40.

While the ITQs are perfectly divisible, and easily transferable, their use and transfers are restricted in some ways, as pointed out in Chapter 1: All transfers of TAC-shares (permanent quotas, in percentages) have to be registered with the Fisheries Directorate. Most transfers of ACEs (quotas over a season, in MT) have to go through the Quota Exchange. The owner of a vessel will lose his quota, measured in cod equivalence, if his vessel harvests less than 50% of the vessel's total quota in two subsequent years. The net transfer of quota from the vessel in any given year must not exceed 50% of her quota. Moreover, no fishing firm may hold more than a given fraction of quotas in each species of fish.

Harvesting Outside Iceland's EEZ

The ITQ system applies, as far as is possible, in those fisheries which either straddle Iceland's EEZ or are outside it. The general rule is that Iceland negotiates with other countries concerned a TAC in each such stock, and then Iceland's share of this TAC is allocated as vessel catch quotas. Capelin and herring are migratory stocks, as previously mentioned, moving in large schools all over the Northeast Atlantic Ocean. Iceland has negotiated a TAC in capelin with Norway and Greenland, by which Iceland receives the bulk of the TAC (since most of the capelin is found and harvested in the Icelandic EEZ). Iceland's share is allocated to individual vessels, on the basis of catch history. The Atlanto-Scandian herring, after the collapse of the late 1960s, suddenly reappeared in the Northeast Atlantic Ocean in 1994, and since then Iceland has negotiated a TAC in this stock with other members of the Northeast Atlantic Fisheries Commission, NEAFC (the Faroese Islands, Norway, the Russian Federation and the European Union). As there was no catch history on which to base initial allocation of quotas, Iceland's share in this TAC (which has usually been about 15% of the TAC) was initially, in 1994-7, not subject to individual quotas but to effort restrictions: entry was free until Iceland's share in the TAC had been reached. On the basis of this catch history, and on vessel hold capacity, vessel catch quotas or ITQs were then allocated for the period 1998-2000.[4]

Iceland has also negotiated within NEAFC a TAC in oceanic redfish which is harvested in the Irminger Sea in international waters southwest of Iceland's EEZ. Since 1997, Iceland's share in the TAC has been allocated as vessel quotas on the basis of catch history (the three best years of the six years in which this fishery

---

4 This was obviously an uneconomical way of allocating the ITQs, since it created an incentive for fishing firms to engage in a 'Derby' for a few years, that is to invest in strategic harvesting in order to establish a catch history. The reason the quotas were not auctioned off was probably that there were already loud demands from some opponents of the ITQ system for auctioning off the existing quotas. The Minister of Fisheries may have felt that by such an auction he would only encourage those people. It is surely ironic if the only impact that supporters of government auctions of quotas have had on policy-making has been to hinder an auction where it may have been justifiable.

had been in operation, with 5% of the total set aside for those who had started the harvesting, a so-called pioneers' quota).

There have been two kinds of disputes between Iceland and other fishing nations in the North Atlantic Ocean. In the deep-sea shrimp fishery which started in 1993 on the Flemish Cap in international waters east of the Canadian EEZ, Iceland has refused to participate in an agreement reached by the North Atlantic Fishing Organisation, NAFO. This is because NAFO tries to manage this fishery by restrictions on effort, i.e. allowable fishing days, to which Iceland is opposed for reasons already explained. Instead, Iceland has since 1997 unilaterally set a TAC for its own fishing vessels on the Flemish Cap; this has then been allocated as ITQs to fishing vessels on the basis of their catch history. The other NAFO countries have accepted this unilateral action, while not endorsing it.

In fishing grounds in international waters in the Barents Sea, the so-called Loophole between Norwegian and Russian territorial waters, Iceland had a dispute with Norway and the Russian Federation from 1993 when Icelandic vessels began to harvest cod there, until May 1999 when the three countries settled their differences, Iceland agreeing to stop harvesting in the Loophole in return for small quotas in Norwegian and Russian territorial waters and an option to buy quotas from Russian vessels and also issuing small quotas to Norway and the Russian Federation in Icelandic waters. During the dispute, Iceland did not try to control the activities of Icelandic trawlers in the Loophole. In 1997-8 however catches there collapsed, as seen in Table 4, at the same time as the TAC in cod in Icelandic waters was increased. Icelandic vessels have therefore largely ceased harvesting fish in the Barents Sea although it made quite a difference in the difficult 1994-5 period.

Table 4
Catch of Icelandic Vessels
Outside Iceland's EEZ 1994-8
(In MT)

	1994	1995	1996	1997	1998
Cod	35,000	34,000	21,800	5,800	2,400
Oceanic redfish	47,100	47,100	51,800	41,000	52,000
Atlanto-Scandian Herring	21,100	173,100	164,600	220,000	197,000
Deep-sea shrimp	2,400	7,600	21,200	6,300	6,800

Source: Fisheries Directorate.

Administration and Enforcement

Two government agencies, under the direction of the Minister of Fisheries, are mainly concerned with administering and enforcing the ITQ system. The Marine Research Institute, (MRI), investigates the state of fish stocks and makes recommendations about annual TACs in different species of fish to the Ministry of Fisheries. The MRI operates research vessels and collects additional information from skippers. It also undertakes basic research in marine biology. The MRI has a staff of about 170; approximately one-third of its costs of operation are covered by its own revenues. The Fisheries Directorate (FD), oversees the day-to-day administration of the ITQ system, especially the collection of data on harvesting and landings. It has a regular staff of about 60; approximately half of its budget is covered by its own revenues. In addition, the FD employs observers for fishing in distant waters, outside Iceland's EEZ.

The ITQ system is in effect enforced by controlling landings. All marine catch is required by law to be weighed on officially approved scales at the point of landing. Municipal authorities operate the weighing stations and collect weighing fees from the vessels to cover their costs. The officials of the weighing stations record the landings and verify species compositions. There are 67 ports under such landings control in Iceland, and major foreign export ports are controlled as well. A sophisticated computer system links ports of landings to the FD, enabling the transmission of daily catch data to the FD's computer department. All catch data are transmitted to the FD twice a day and processed for dissemination, by several means, through the FD's Web pages, through monthly publications and by phone to skippers and vessel owners checking their catch status. Status reports are sent to vessel owners regularly and upon request. The FD's Web pages of fisheries data show in detail the catch status of individual vessels, quota transfers between different vessels or in different species, quota shares and landings.

A third government agency, The Icelandic Coast Guard, under the direction of the Minister of Justice, and with a staff of about 130, monitors fishing vessels at sea and enforces regional closures, with gunboats, helicopters and aeroplanes. As already mentioned, extensive nursery grounds are permanently closed to fishing vessels, and the spawning grounds of cod are closed for a few weeks in late winter during the spawning period. Moreover, the Minister of Fisheries, on the advice of the MRI, has the right of immediate, temporary closure of areas with excessive juvenile fish. There is also a 12 miles limit for large trawlers in most areas.

In addition to the surveillance provided by the FD and the Coast Guard, the Ministry of Fisheries itself employs a group of observers of fishing in the Icelandic waters, some of whom take trips on fishing vessels and some of whom travel between ports of landings. Those observers try to ensure compliance with regulations on mesh size, bycatches, and so on. Mesh size has to be 135 mm or equivalent, for example, and in the shrimp fishery a sorting grid is mandatory to avoid the bycatch of juvenile fish. In the demersal fisheries devices for excluding juveniles are also mandatory in certain areas.

The Ministry of Fisheries itself has an office staff of about 20. The Ministry charges holders of ITQs a low fee for the costs of administering and enforcing the ITQ system, with an upper limit of 0.4% of the estimated catch value. The revenue from the fee is about US$8-9 millions a year, and in addition there is revenue from a fee for fishing permits of about US$2 millions a year.

The total net costs of enforcing and administering the ITQ-system, less than US$30 millions a year, including basic marine biology research and guarding the territorial waters, do not seem huge in comparison to the total catch value in the Icelandic fisheries which is, in the late 1990s, on average about US$800 millions a year. Violations of the Fisheries Management Act and the corresponding Ministry of Fisheries regulations carry heavy penalties, such as fines, expropriation of catch and gear and cancellation of fishing permits. While the Ministry of Fisheries has wide discretionary powers in assessing such penalties and a proven willingness to use them, alleged violators have recourse to the courts if unsatisfied with the Ministry's decisions.

Are the Icelandic ITQs Property Rights?

On land, fencing techniques such as barbed wire have enabled individuals to establish property rights in (that is, to exclude others from the utilisation of) land and other immovable objects, whereas branding techniques have enabled them to establish property rights in (that is, again to exclude others from the utilisation of) animals and other movable objects. Fences can however hardly be erected around different areas of the deep sea (although some kinds of fencing may be possible in inshore fisheries), and it is also difficult to see how individual fish in the sea can be branded (at least cod, herring and other species of fish that the Icelanders harvest).

It may be argued therefore that ITQs are substitutes for property rights based either on fencing or branding. They are not exclusive rights to the utilisation of particular areas of the sea, or of particular fish, but rather exclusive rights to harvest a given share of a given total catch of a species of fish. They are rights of extraction rather than property, comparable to rights to extract a certain quantity of timber from a given forest, or to harvest a certain number of deer from a given colony (Hannesson, 1994). While such rights provide incentives to cut the timber and to catch the deer in the most efficient ways, they may not be sufficiently strong to provide the optimal husbandry of the forest or the deer colony.

Nevertheless, ITQs, as described in the fisheries economics literature, have many of the efficient features of individual property rights. They are exclusive, individual, divisible, transferable and permanent. One important feature is that the permanent ITQs, that is, TAC-shares, are share-rights: they are (transferable) rights to harvest, say, 0.1% of the total allowable catch in a species of fish in the foreseeable future. Holders of such rights have a clear interest in the long-term profitability of the resource. There would be a crucial difference in the behaviour of two groups of quota holders, where the members of one group would each have a permanent quota expressed in a given quantity of fish, for example, 250 MT of cod a year, whereas the members of the other groups would each have a permanent quota expressed in a given share of the total catch, for example, 0.1% of the TAC in cod. The latter group would be concerned not only with minimising harvesting costs, but also with setting the TAC in such a way that the long-term profitability of the fish stock in question would be maximised.

Arguably, ITQs, as described in the fisheries economics literature, come as near to being private property rights as is simply feasible in deep-sea fisheries. But what about the Icelandic ITQs, described in this and the preceding Chapter? Those ITQs are certainly individual and divisible. They are also exclusive although their exclusivity is somewhat reduced by the continuing existence of exemptions from the system for some boats, under 6 MT. But it is a minor exemption and sooner or later all small boats will probably be integrated into the ITQ system. The Icelandic ITQs are also mostly transferable: the restrictions on quota transfers are not very important. Nevertheless, they are restrictions.

For the system to be more efficient, most economists would argue, ITQs should not be issued to fishing vessels, but to individuals and firms and they should be freely transferable. No restrictions should be imposed either on the relative or absolute amount each individual firm could hold, as is now the case. The ITQs should also be fully recognised by the law as possible collaterals which they are not at the moment. There should not be conditions on their use, either, such as the rules described in Chapter 1 to discourage speculation in ITQs. More speculation would facilitate transfers in the ITQ market, hasten the reduction of the fishing fleet and enable quota holders to be more flexible in their operations.

The main problem in the Icelandic fisheries is, however, that the ITQs, even if issued to individual vessels for an indefinite period of time since 1990, are not really permanent and secure. As described in Chapter 1, in the 1990 Fisheries Management Act, a paragraph was inserted to the effect that no assignment of ITQs by this law could constitute any permanent property rights to such quotas or become the ground for compensation if the quotas were taken from their holders. While it is unlikely that the ITQ system would be abolished, or the quotas taken from their present holders, especially since in early 2000, only 19% of the quotas are still in the hands of those to whom they were initially assigned, the unwillingness of the Icelandic Parliament to take any steps legally to recognise the ITQs as property rights, even if they are taxed as such and to all purposes treated as such, has added to the uncertainty facing their holders.

Concluding Remarks

The emergence of ITQs in the Icelandic fisheries has interesting similarities to the emergence of property rights amongst Indians in Labrador, as analysed by Harold Demsetz (1967). For centuries, before the arrival of Europeans, the Indians had hunted beaver primarily for food and the few furs they needed. Since the beaver stock was a non-exclusive resource, the Indians did not have a vested interest in increasing or maintaining it. However, as their needs were small and the technology primitive the negative effects of beaver hunting were insignificant. When European traders arrived, hunting technology improved, and demand for furs greatly increased. The scale of hunting increased so the harmful effects which each hunter had on others by his hunting became significant. Consequently, the Indians divided themselves into several bands in order to hunt more efficiently. Each band appropriated pieces of land, roughly similar in quality, for it to hunt exclusively. By the middle of the 18th century, the privately allotted territories were relatively stabilised. Thus, the fur trade had encouraged the husbanding of beavers and the prevention of poaching which such husbanding requires.

Demsetz tells this tale to illustrate his main point about property rights. They emerge when harmful or beneficial effects of economic activity emerge, enabling individuals to take them into account. Consider pollution, mentioned in Chapter 1. If I pollute a river in which you swim, or fish salmon, or from which you get your drinking water, with the consequence that you cannot continue your use of the river, it is typically because neither you nor anyone else owns the river, being able to hold me responsible for my activities. While the pollution I cause harms you, it does not cost me anything.

The solution would seem to be to define property rights to the river, just as the Labrador Indians established property rights in different pieces of land. Sometimes, however, the definition of property rights is not feasible: the costs of establishing them are higher than the gains. Demsetz points out that the Indians of the Southwest plains who came into contact with the European market at the same time as the Labrador Indians, did not establish new property rights in response to increased demand for the animals they hunted and improved hunting technology. The reason was that the animals of the plains, such as the buffalo, were primarily grazing animals wandering over wide areas. The cost of husbanding those animals (fencing or branding) was therefore much higher (at least until the introduction of barbed wire) than the cost of husbanding beavers in Labrador which were confined to relatively small areas.

The pelagic species of fish in the Icelandic waters, herring and capelin, are rather similar to the animals of the Southwest plains described by Demsetz: clearly, any territorial rights to those two fish stocks would not have been feasible. Neither fencing nor branding would have been possible. On the other hand, cod and other demersal fish are similar to beavers in the Labrador forests in that they are relatively territorial. The fishing grounds where those species are found are known and rather well-defined. Unlike branding, fencing would in theory have been possible in the demersal fisheries (and even more in the inshore shrimp and nephrops fisheries, confined to small and clearly demarcated areas).

The interesting question is then why territorial rights were not established in those stocks. Several answers may be suggested. First, there were hardly any legal precedents or possibilities available to fishing vessel owners or legislators. While non-territorial fishing rights in the form of ITQs had already been tried in the pelagic fisheries, and seen to work, ideas about property rights in areas of the sea would have been dismissed as pure fantasy. Second, demersal fishing grounds are very large in scale, creating possible economic inefficiencies of their own as independent units of operations, while vessel catch quotas are perfectly divisible. Third, fencing each fishing ground off would have been quite costly. Instead, under the ITQ system only the Icelandic EEZ is really fenced off. Moreover, the Icelandic fishing fleet includes many multi-purpose vessels, so it was economical to have a comprehensive quota system within which a vessel might switch from harvesting one species to another without many problems. It is also convenient that the quotas are expressed in terms of cod equivalence so fishing vessels can easily solve the problem of bycatch.

On the whole, the evolution of the Icelandic ITQ system can be interpreted as the practical response to the problem of vessel owners imposing economic costs on one another by excessive fishing effort and over-capitalisation—costs which should not be blamed on them, but rather on the lack of property rights and thus the lack of information about those costs (Coase, 1960). It amounts to the enclosure of the fish stocks in Icelandic waters—an enclosure not yet completed.

3. The Performance of the ITQ System

When access to a resource such as the fish stocks in Icelandic waters suddenly becomes exclusive, the behaviour of those utilising the resource should be expected greatly to change. When an ITQ system is introduced in deep-sea fisheries the fish stocks in question are taken into custody, so to speak, by the quota holders. Certainly there has been a marked change in the behaviour of Icelandic vessel owners since the introduction of the ITQ system. Even if their rights of extraction from the fish stocks are by no means as clear or certain as they could be, quota holders within the powerful Association of Fishing Vessel Owners have begun to look upon themselves as custodians of the fish stocks, taking a long-term view of their utilisation, and strongly supporting a cautious approach to the setting of TACs.

Since the introduction of the ITQ system, slowly most stocks in Icelandic waters have become stronger, in particular the valuable cod stock (at the same time as this stock has collapsed in some other parts of the world). While the reduction of the Icelandic fishing fleet has not been as rapid as many hoped in the first years of the ITQ system, fishing effort has gone down, especially in the pelagic fisheries, and there has been considerable readjustment in the fishing sector. Unprofitable firms have gone out of business, while other firms have merged, and rationalised their operations, with many of them becoming public corporations. While fewer fishing firms therefore hold quotas now than in the beginning, there are many more owners of the remaining firms.

In short, the years since the introduction of vessel catch quotas have seen the growing commercialisation of the Icelandic fisheries. Many were initially concerned that this would mean a net transfer of quotas from the small fishing villages scattered around the coastline, to the urbanised Southwest of Iceland, but this has not been the case. Indeed, there has been a net transfer of quotas from the Southwest. Problems remain in the fisheries, mainly concerning highgrading and the uncertain status of the ITQs. But on the whole, the ITQ system has performed well (Runolfsson, 1999).

The Pelagic and the Small Fisheries

ITQs have been applied much longer in the pelagic fisheries than in the demersal fisheries, from 1975 in the herring fishery and from 1980 in the capelin fishery. The evidence is quite clear in those two fisheries. Since 1975, herring catches have increased almost tenfold while fishing effort has not increased; indeed, it has decreased. The number of vessels in the herring fishery has gone down from about 65 in 1975 to about 30-40 in the 1990s. Catch per unit of effort in the herring fishery is now roughly 10 times higher than it was when ITQs were first issued. Two herring stocks are harvested by Icelandic vessels, the Icelandic summer spawning stock, and the Atlanto-Scandian stock (partly outside Iceland's EEZ). Both have gained in strength in the last few years. Marine biologists estimate the herring stock biomass to be bigger now than it has been since the 1950s.

While capelin catches fluctuate from one year to another, there is no clear downward trend in capelin catches. But the number of vessels (specialised purse seine vessels) in the capelin fishery have gone down, from 68 in 1979 to 44 in 1996. The fleet total tonnage (GRT) has been reduced by over 25% and total days at sea for the fleet by almost 25%. Efficiency thus seems to have significantly increased in the capelin fishery. The development in the two pelagic fisheries, in terms of catch per unit of fleet, is shown in Figure 3.

Figure 3
CPUF for the Purse Seine Fleet
in the Pelagic Fisheries 1977-97
Source: National Bureau of Statistics

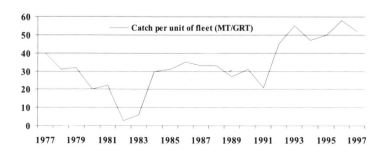

45

The evidence in the much smaller, but quite valuable nephrops, shrimp and scallop fisheries is not as clear and dramatic as in the pelagic fisheries, because there was never a radical change of the system under which those species were harvested. There was never non-exclusive access to those fisheries: they are mostly inshore fisheries, utilised by local communities, and only developed in the late 1960s. However, the number of boats has been significantly reduced in those fisheries, whereas there has been no clear trend, upwards or downwards, in total catches. In the last decade or so, the number of nephrops boats has gone down from 57 to 42, of inshore shrimp boats from 60 to 44 and scallop boats from 21 to 15. Efficiency seems, on the whole, to have increased although, to repeat, over-utilisation because of non-exclusive access was never as much a problem there as in other Icelandic fisheries.

The Demersal Fisheries

The evidence is less clear in the demersal fisheries, subject to vessel catch quotas since 1984. Even if Figure 4 shows that increases in fishing capital came to a halt in 1984-5, this can be ascribed to heavy losses in the demersal fisheries no less than to the introduction of quotas. In 1986 fishing capital indeed started to increase again, although it has been slowly decreasing since 1989. At the same time, TACs in the demersal fisheries were lower than previously.

This does not mean, however, that efficiency has not increased significantly in the demersal fisheries. There are important factors explaining the temporary increase in fishing capital in 1986-9 and the rather slow decrease after that. The two major factors were the existence of the mixed system of effort restrictions, encouraging investment, and vessel catch quotas, discouraging investment, in 1985-90; and the exemption of small boats from the system, first those under 10 GRT, then those under 6 GRT. Indeed, in 1984-1990 the number of fishing boats under 10 GRT almost doubled, from 828 to 1,599. In 1991, this trend was to some extent reversed, and in 1997 boats under 10 GRT numbered 1,114. A third factor was the installation of freezing equipment in the big trawlers. In 1983, there were only three freezer trawlers, in 1990 they were 28, and in 1997 they were 54. This was not really an increase in fishing capital, but rather a structural change, the transfer of fish processing from land to sea. Yet another factor was that specialised trawlers were in the mid-1980s bought for the emerging deep-sea shrimp fishery, not subject to quotas until 1988.

A fifth factor which should be mentioned is that a significant proportion of the deep-sea trawler fleet was due for replacement by the mid-1980s. The years 1986-7 were profitable for fishing firms many of which therefore used the opportunity to replace their ageing vessels. Moreover, modern standards of accommodation for the crew require much more space than old trawlers and boats could offer. Also, because of an increase in the export of fresh fish on ice, in special containers aboard fishing vessels, newer vessels have been built with more storage space than the old ones had. Firms in the demersal fisheries may have been reluctant to divest their fishing capital for yet another reason. They probably expect that with the recovery of the fish stocks in Icelandic waters, TACs in cod and other demersal species will eventually be increased. After all, in 1997 the total catch of cod in the Icelandic waters was less than half of what it had been sixteen years earlier. Moreover, in the mid-1990s some firms may have been investing in strategic harvesting, creating a basis for claims in shares of possible future TACs in fisheries outside Iceland's territorial waters. Those firms may have been preparing for an eventual opportunity to harvest fish in distant waters.

Figure 4
Demersal Fishing Effort and Capital 1979-1997
(index 1979=100). Source: National Bureau of Statistics

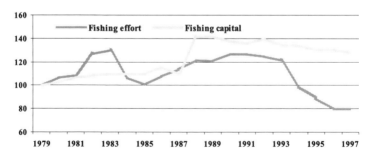

For all those reasons, fishing capital has decreased rather slowly since 1989. Fishing effort, defined as volume in GRT times fishing days, has also decreased, as can be seen from Figure 4, with the exception of the period 1986-91; this temporary increase can be explained partly by the existence of effort restrictions and partly by the decline in the demersal stocks (and lower TACs), making harvesting more difficult. Since 1991, however, fishing effort in the demersal fisheries has been substantially reduced, at a faster rate than the fall in catch value. There is little question that this is mainly because of the ITQ system. It has induced fishing firms to organise their harvesting more economically. It should be noted that catch value in the demersal fisheries has not gone down as dramatically as the total catch itself. This is not only because of price increases, but also because harvesting in the ITQ system has become better organised than it was under the previous effort restrictions: vessels try to catch the fish at the time when demand is at its highest, and so on. Trends in catch value, fishing capital and fishing effort in Iceland's demersal fisheries indicate that efficiency has increased considerably, especially after the ITQ system was made comprehensive in 1990-1.

This conclusion is strengthened by observing the simple and undisputed fact that most Icelandic fishing firms have, since the introduction of the ITQ system, become profitable whereas previously most of them made heavy losses. Yet another method of evaluating the performance of the system is to observe the market prices of quotas. According to an estimate by an Icelandic economist of the trend in 1984-95 (Arnason 1996), the price range of cod quotas in this period went up from US$ 55-87 per MT to US$ 1,050-1,389 per MT. The total value of quotas went, in the same period, up from US$ 36-57 millions to US$ 235-275 millions. While those figures have to be taken with some caution, they show that considerable economic rent is being derived from the demersal fisheries in Iceland and that this rent is increasing.

The Impact on Regional Development

One of the most sensitive issues in Icelandic politics is regional development. Numerous attempts have been made to halt the migration of people to the Southwest—to Reykjavik and its environs—such as the establishment of special regional funds to stimulate economic development outside the Southwest. These

48

attempts have met with little or no success: the bulk of the population lives in or near Reykjavik. When the ITQ system was introduced, there was some concern that quotas would be transferred to the Southwest. The result would be, it was argued, unemployment in the small fishing villages scattered along the coastline, and an acceleration in the ongoing migration to the Southwest. Indeed, to hinder such a development some politicians proposed regional quotas—quotas transferable only within a region.

Figure 5 – The Regions of Iceland

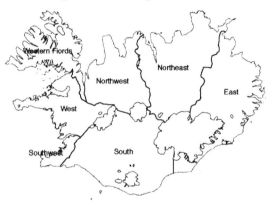

To allay such fears certain restrictions were imposed on the transfers of ACEs between regions, as we have seen, while transfers of TAC-shares were not subject to similar restrictions. In practice, these restrictions have not had a significant impact on the workings of the ITQ system. One reason may be that the ITQ system has had an effect on regional development opposite to what was feared. On the whole, it has strengthened the economy in the fishing villages, although firms in those villages are operated with varying degrees of success, as is to be expected. Figure 5 shows the seven main regions in Iceland, and Table 5 the development of quota holdings in those regions. The really important fact is that the Southwest which in 1984 held 29.7% of the total quota (in cod equivalents), in the fishing year 1998/9 only held 25.7 %. There has been a net quota transfer to three regions, the West, the Northwest and, in particular, the Northeast, and an almost negligible net quota transfer from other three regions, the South, the Western Fjords and the East.

Table 5
Share of Quota Holdings by Regions, 1984-99[5]
%

	South-west	West	Western fjords	North-west	North-east	East	South
1984	29.7	9.0	13.6	6.1	14.9	13.2	13.5
1985	29.3	9.0	13.6	6.3	15.1	13.3	13.5
1986	27.8	9.7	13.9	6.3	14.8	13.7	13.8
1987	24.9	9.9	14.1	6.9	16.9	13.7	13.6
1988	24.6	9.6	14.2	7.4	16.7	13.5	14.0
1989	22.8	9.3	14.7	7.9	17.5	13.2	14.6
1990	24.1	9.0	14.0	7.7	17.1	12.9	15.2
1991	23.6	9.4	14.0	7.9	17.9	12.6	14.6
1991/92	23.6	9.9	14.0	6.9	18.5	14.0	13.1
1992/93	23.2	19.9	13.5	7.2	18.9	13.6	13.8
1993/94	24.2	10.0	12.3	7.0	18.5	13.9	14.1
1994/95	24.8	10.0	11.7	7.1	19.0	12.8	14.6
1995/96	25.6	10.1	11.6	7.6	20.2	12.0	13.0
1996/97	25.5	10.0	12.3	8.3	20.5	11.3	12.1
1997/98	23.8	11.7	10.6	7.0	21.9	12.0	12.1
1998/99	25.7	12.4	9.6	8.4	21.2	11.1	11.6
Average	25.2	9.9	13.0	7.3	18.1	12.9	13.6

Source: Fisheries Directorate.

While this is certainly remarkable, quota holdings do not tell the whole story. Another important indicator of regional development should be the pattern of demersal landings, shown in Table 6. Since the introduction of the ITQ system, landings have increased most in the Northeast, as have quota holdings, but there has been a slight increase in landings in the Southwest despite its smaller share of quota holdings. One explanation is that wetfish floor markets were first introduced in the Southwest, and the first three such markets are located there. Moreover, the regional distribution of freezer trawlers (where fish processing is essentially moved aboard) tends to alter the story: they are mainly located in the Southwest and in the North. Another divergence is that landings have decreased in

---

5   In cod equivalents, for cod, haddock, saithe, redfish and Greenland halibut, at registered port of vessel.

the South despite its almost unchanged relative quota holdings. The explanation for this is that vessels in the South tend to land their catches abroad to a greater extent than vessels in other regions.

Nevertheless, these figures tell the same overall story. There has not been a significant transfer of resources to the Southwest from the rest of the country, as was feared in the first years of the ITQ system. On the contrary, the ITQ system seems to be accomplishing what numerous regional funds in Iceland never managed to do: to provide people in the fishing villages scattered along the coastline with feasible economic opportunities. It should be noted, moreover, that the prevailing regional distribution of quotas has some interesting political consequences. If a special tax were imposed on quota holders in order to extract the rent from the fisheries, as some Icelanders have proposed, then this tax would probably mean a transfer of resources to the Southwest from the rest of the country. While about 75% of the quotas are held outside the Southwest, about 75% of the population resides in the Southwest. This may become a powerful factor in a possible political conflict over rent expropriation in the fisheries, discussed in Chapter 4.

Table 6
Share of Demersal Landings by Regions, 1983-98[6]
%

	South-west	West	Western fjords	North-west	North-east	East	South
1983	27.9	11.2	13.4	5.3	14.3	13.7	14.2
1984	26.5	10.9	15.3	6.1	14.6	13.0	13.6
1985	25.3	11.0	13.6	6.8	15.9	14.3	13.1
1986	25.2	11.8	13.2	6.8	16.8	15.2	11.0
1987	25.4	12.0	12.7	7.7	17.4	15.1	9.7
1988	25.8	10.2	13.8	7.3	19.5	14.1	9.3
1989	27.3	10.4	13.6	6.5	19.2	13.0	10.0
1990	29.7	9.4	12.4	7.6	20.1	11.2	9.6
1991	30.4	8.9	13.0	7.8	20.0	11.3	8.6
1992	30.6	7.7	13.2	7.9	20.7	11.6	8.3
1993	30.6	8.8	12.7	7.8	21.8	10.1	8.2
1994	34.3	7.9	11.8	6.4	20.3	10.7	8.7
1995	34.2	10.3	12.4	4.4	17.2	12.5	8.9
1996	27.3	10.4	13.6	6.5	19.2	13.0	10.0
1997	32.1	12.8	12.0	4.2	16.5	12.4	10.1
1998	30.9	13.1	13.0	4.2	16.7	12.0	10.2
Average	28.9	10.3	13.1	6.6	18.3	12.8	10.2

Source: Fisheries Directorate.

Concentration of ITQs?

Another sensitive issue in the Icelandic economy is the structure of the fisheries sector, especially the relative size of fishing firms. Has the ITQ system led to concentration in the fisheries? The answer must be yes. The objective of the change to an ITQ system was the reduction of fishing capital and fishing effort per catch, and this would most likely, although not inevitably, lead to a reduction in the number of fishing firms, and hence to increased concentration, as conventionally measured. The question has therefore to be rephrased. Apart from the inevitable reduction in the number of fishing vessels and fishing firms, brought about by quota

---

6 In cod equivalents, for cod, haddock, saithe, redfish and Greenland halibut; as a fraction of demersal landings for domestic processing.

transactions, is a further tendency to market concentration discernible in the fisheries?

It is difficult to evaluate the existing data. Certainly, many fishing firms have merged, and others have gone out of business. Table 7 shows that in the fishing year 1991/2 the ten largest firms in the demersal fisheries held 24.6% of the total demersal quotas. In the fishing year 1998/9, however, the ten largest firms in those fisheries held 37.6% of the total quotas. This is indeed a significant increase. But the concentration in the Icelandic fisheries after the introduction of the quota system is probably no more than was to be expected. What is important is that no one fishing firm is in a dominant position. The two largest firms in the demersal fisheries, Utgerdarfelag Akureyringa and Samherji, both in the Northeast, each held 5.5% of the total demersal quotas in 1998/9. The 10th largest fishing firm held only 2.3% of the total quotas. The quotas are in other words widely dispersed. It is interesting that one of the largest fishing firms, Samherji, in late 1983 when ITQs were first issued in the demersal fisheries, had only one significant asset, a deep-sea trawler. Under the ITQ system, however, the firm has grown rapidly, operating in the late 1990s no less than 20 vessels from four countries, two shrimp processing plants, two reduction plants, one freezing plant and a marketing office in England. This would seem to be an example of the possibility for successful entrepreneurs of entering the ITQ system.

Table 7
Quota Shares of Largest Harvesting Firms
in the Demersal Fisheries 1991-9[7]
% (ranking)

Harvesting firm (all Ltd.)	91/92	92/93	93/94	94/95	95/96	96/97	97/98	98/99
UA (NE)	4.0 (2)	4.6 (2)	4.6 (2)	5.0 (2)	5.4 (2)	5.4 (2)	5.0 (2)	5.5 (1)
Samherji (NE)	3.2 (3)	3.4 (3)	3.4 (3)	3.5 (3)	3.6 (3)	4.2 (3)	5.6 (1)	5.5 (2)
Grandi (SW)	4.3 (1)	4.9 (1)	4.9 (1)	5.1 (1)	6.1 (1)	5.7 (1)	4.9 (3)	4.8 (3)
Har. Bodvarsson (W)	2.2 (6)	2.3 (5)	2.3 (6)	2.3 (5)	2.6 (5)	3.3 (5)	4.5 (4)	4.3 (4)
Thorm. rammi (NW)							4.0 (6)	3.8 (5)
Vinnslustodin (S)	2.5 (4)	2.0 (6)	2.9 (4)	2.5 (4)	2.2 (7)	2.0 (8)	4.3 (5)	3.3 (6)
Skagfirdingur (NW)	1.5 (9)	1.5 (10)	1.7 (8)	2.2 (7)	2.9 (4)	3.3 (4)	2.8 (8)	3.2 (7)
Snaefell (NE)								2.6 (8)
Thorbjorn (SW)							2.5 (7)	2.3 (9)
Basafell (Wfj)							2.3 (9)	2.3 (10)
Total of 10 largest	24.6	25.9	27.0	28.2	30.7	31.8	38.1	37.6

Source: Fisheries Directorate

Moreover, it is misleading to say that the ITQs have been concentrated in fewer hands, because the largest firms holding ITQs have become public corporations and have in this way come under the ownership of many more people than before. The great dispersal of ownership of the largest fishing firms is shown in Table 8. Altogether, there are about 10-20,000 shareholders in Icelandic fishing firms, and there seems to be a development towards a further dispersal of ownership. The Icelanders see good investment opportunities in the big fishing firms which, in turn, use the additional capital to rationalise their operations (and, in some cases, to extend them to fisheries in other countries). Hence, no individual in Iceland can therefore be said to control more than a fraction of the total quota.

---

7 Shares of total cod equivalent values for each year. Quota holdings in cod, haddock, saithe, redfish, Greenland halibut and plaice as percentage of total allotments of cod, haddock, saithe and redfish.

Table 8
Distribution of Stock
in Ten Largest Demersal Harvesting Firms
in November 1998

Harvesting firm	ITQs 1998 /99	No. of stock-holders	Group 1	Group 2	Others	Biggest stockholders: 1	3	5	10
Samherji	5.7	3,864	9	1	89	21	62	76	80
UA	5.3	1,720	35	49	16	20	50	64	76
Grandi	4.8	1,080	18	21	61	26	47	57	71
Har. Bodvarsson	4.3	1,227	19	37	44	10	24	37	59
Thorm. rammi	3.8	580	18	23	59	19	35	42	61
Vinnslustodin	3.3	762	17	35	48	18	38	48	67
Skagfirdingur	3.2	197	22	8	70	56	74	87	94
Snaefell	2.6	119	3	96	1	92	96	98	99
Thorbjorn	2.3	368	6	11	83	11	34	51	71
Basafell	2.3	332	18	27	55	24	39	48	64
Total	37.6	10,049							

Group 1: Municipalities, cooperatives, pension funds, stock funds, etc.
Group 2: Corporations and cooperatives listed on the Icelandic stock exchange.

Remaining Problems

This brief review suggests that the ITQ system in the Icelandic fisheries has performed as well as could be expected, and without any serious social consequences. However, some problems remain. Some of them are institutional and can be corrected, but probably at a some political cost: the partial exemption of small boats from the system, some remaining restrictions on transfers, and the uncertain legal status of the quotas.

But a further problem does not lie in the institutions or rules that apply to the Icelandic fisheries, but rather in the fact that all quotas have to be expressed in metric tonnes over the fishing season whereas the values of two tonnes are not always equal, either because they come from different species of fish or because specimens of one species differ in value. Discarding may therefore occur. However, bycatches, the throwing away of non-targeted species, are not much of a problem in the Icelandic ITQ system because a quota in one species is easily transferred to a quota in another species, and they have a common denominator, namely cod.

Highgrading, the throwing away of specimens of the targeted species, usually because they are too small to be of much value, seems to be a greater problem, even if its extent is probably exaggerated by critics of the ITQ system. In a 1993 report by a government commission on highgrading in the demersal fisheries, it was estimated to range from 1 to 6% of total catch volume depending on the types of gear and vessels used (Arnason, 1994). Moreover, according to the report there had been no detectable increase in highgrading since the introduction of the ITQ system. One reason for the relative insignificance of highgrading is undoubtedly the strict surveillance of fishing vessels. It should also be pointed out that highgrading is caused because it is quite difficult to differentiate in harvesting instead of in landing between specimens of different value. In the future, hopefully, improvements in fishing gear will enable skippers and their crew to differentiate more fully than now between such specimens.

Another interesting problem has appeared in the Icelandic fisheries in the 1990s. If one stock of fish is excessively harvested, another stock competing with it for food may grow disproportionately large. The ecological balance has been disturbed. It is therefore important to take a multi-species approach to the fisheries.

The most important marine mammal in Icelandic waters is the whale. In the first decades of the 20th century when whaling by foreign fleets had driven various whale stocks to the brink of extinction, Iceland imposed a moratorium on the whaling industry, and only resumed harvesting whales when the stocks had strengthened. But in 1985 the International Whaling Commission decided on a moratorium on commercial whaling. Iceland had to comply with it, even if marine biologists presented evidence to the effect that the stocks harvested in Icelandic waters—fin, sei and minke whales—were not in any danger. The reason for Iceland's compliance with the ban on whaling was not least the fear of adverse reactions in its best markets for fish products, such as Germany and the United States.

Subsequently, however, research has shown a large growth in the whale population in Icelandic waters. It is even more evident now than in 1985 that limited harvesting would not put the fin, sei and minke whale stocks at risk. Moreover, the size of the whale stocks can have considerable effect on the productivity of the fish stocks in Icelandic waters. It has been estimated by Icelandic marine biologists, for example, that if the whale stocks in Icelandic waters increase to the level of 40 years ago, the productivity of the cod stock is likely to become 10% less than it would otherwise have been. The problem is, to put it bluntly, that whales (and for that matter also seals) are competing with man for the fish in the North Atlantic Ocean. A strong argument can therefore be made for lifting the ban on whaling, not only because a valuable resource is not being utilised, but also because it may be necessary to maintain balance within the marine ecosystem.

4. Current Controversies

While the Icelandic fisheries present a strikingly different picture from those in many neighbouring countries, whose fisheries are loss-making, heavily dependent on government subsidies and often even depleting fish stocks, the ITQ system is still quite controversial in Iceland. Its most unpopular aspect is the transferability of quotas. Regularly, there is a public outcry when a holder of a quota sells it, even if this can be seen as a positive step, since it means that the seller leaves the over- capitalised fisheries: this is readjustment by trade, not by force.

But in public debate, some more general philosophical objections are raised to the ITQ system. One common objection is based on the fact that it means at least the partial enclosure of fish stocks. It implies the development of exclusive extraction rights to fish stocks which share some important features of private property rights, as we have seen. It is argued that the initial allocation of quotas at the end of 1983 in the demersal fisheries was unjust because it constituted a gift to their recipients—owners of fishing vessels operating in the three preceding years—excluding all others. The critics of the ITQ system say that the fish stocks in Icelandic waters are the declared common property of the Icelandic nation, and that it is therefore unjust that individual fishing firms should reap the profit of utilising them. They propose either that the quotas should be taken from their present holders and auctioned off by government, or that a special tax should be imposed on their holders, designed to capture the rent which can be derived from the resource.

This being said, the opposition in Iceland to the ITQ system has probably been no stronger than was to be expected in a country so dependent on fishing. In Iceland, almost everyone lives in some ways close to the fisheries, and everything which happens there is well reported in the media, whereas in most other countries fishing is marginal to the economy and usually given scant attention in public debate. Therefore, less opposition should be expected from the general public in most other countries to the introduction of ITQ systems in fisheries.

Is the ITQ System Unjust?

The arguments against the initial allocation of quotas are directed solely at the allocation of quotas in the demersal fisheries at the end of 1983. It would seem that if that was unjust, so was the initial allocation of quotas in the pelagic fisheries in 1975-80 and in the small nephrops, shrimp and scallops fisheries in the 1970s. It is however difficult to see how the demersal quotas could have been allocated in any other way than on the basis of catch history.

The task was, to return to our illustration of the fisheries problem in Chapter 1, to reduce the fishing fleet from sixteen to eight boats. While in theory this could be done by government either taxing or pricing eight boats out, in practice it could only be done by assigning quotas sufficient for the successful operation of eight boats to the existing sixteen boats, making them transferable so that the more efficient could over time buy out those who wanted to leave the fisheries, because of old age, better opportunities elsewhere or for other reasons. In this way, and in this way only, could the necessary adjustment take place peacefully. After all, vessel owners had invested in their vessels, gear and practical knowledge (human capital), in the belief that the fishing grounds in Icelandic waters would remain open to them. When it was necessary to restrict access, it seemed natural to restrict it to those who had made such investments because they were the only ones to lose from the restriction, not those who had not made any such investments. It was easier (less costly) not to enter the fisheries than to leave them.

Putting it differently, this was the only Pareto-efficient change. A change in institutions is Pareto-efficient if (a) all benefit from it, or (b) some benefit, and no one loses (Buchanan, 1959). If government had auctioned off the quotas, it would itself have benefited. Those eight boat owners who would have been able to purchase quotas would have neither benefited nor lost. But those eight who would have been outbid at the auction would have lost, because their capital, quite specific to the fisheries, would have become almost worthless overnight. On the other hand, when quotas were assigned to the existing owners of fishing capital, and made transferable, as was done, no one lost. Those eight boat owners who would, over time, have bought quotas from the other eight boat owners, would have benefited. Those eight boat owners who would have sold their quotas and left the fisheries would also have benefited. Even government would have benefited by the increased productivity in the fisheries, in the form of higher tax revenues. The crew of the eight boats which would have had to leave the fisheries would under an initial assignment of quotas to vessel owners have had a much longer adjustment period than under a government auction which would have made them redundant overnight. Their skills were not anyway specific to fisheries; they could therefore seek employment elsewhere without losing much of their bargaining power.

By the initial allocation of catch quotas on the basis of catch history, no one was harmed. On the contrary, a system of rules was developed under which a group of people who had been imposing economic costs on one another by over-utilising the fish stocks in Icelandic waters, could in transactions put an end to this. Unlike pollution, however, the harm was invisible: it was benefit foregone, the possible rent from a fertile resource which had been dissipated in over-capitalisation and excessive fishing effort.

The ITQ system was, to use economic jargon, a way of internalising an externality. Its introduction consisted in assigning responsibility for the fish stocks to individuals and thus enabling them to eliminate the harmful effects that they had previously had on one another by their activities. It is therefore misleading to speak about a 'special gift' to the owners of vessels in the demersal fisheries when they received vessel catch quotas at the end of 1983. What government did for them was what it had previously neglected to do, and what is usually regarded as its duty: to define and uphold a system of rules under which people could settle their differences peacefully and to mutual advantage. This system of rules certainly enabled Icelandic vessel owners to create wealth, but this is precisely what property is supposed to do.

At this point, opponents of the Icelandic ITQ system may

however point to the declaration, in the 1990 Fisheries Management Act, about the fish stocks being the common property of the Icelandic nation. It is an interesting question what this declaration, inserted at a late stage in the evolution of the ITQ system to facilitate a vote in the legislature, precisely means. Legal experts in Iceland answer that the concept of 'common property' is rather vague (Lindal, 1998). They say that this declaration should not be interpreted as if the fish stocks belonged to government like some buildings and cars in Iceland do. It should be regarded, rather, as a declaration to the effect that Iceland has full jurisdiction over the fish stocks in Icelandic waters and that their utilisation have to serve the long-term interests of the Icelandic nation. Certainly, they say, legislators did not mean to nationalise the fish stocks by inserting this declaration into the Fisheries Management Act.

The Demand For a Resource Rent Tax

Some Icelandic economists have argued for a special resource rent tax in the fisheries, on the grounds that such a tax would not have any distortional effects, unlike most other taxes, that the owners of fishing vessels do not deserve the rent from the fish stocks, and that such a tax might make ITQs more acceptable to the general public (Gylfason, 1990; Moller, 1996).

It should be pointed out that unlike pollution fees, for example, such a tax would not be corrective (serve to internalise an externality, to use economic jargon again). The ITQ system has already accomplished the necessary correction by enabling vessel owners to reduce fishing capital and fishing effort in their transactions to the most profitable level. The proposed resource rent tax would therefore be redistributive. While a resource rent tax might seem plausible, if it could replace other more distortional taxes, it is quite optimistic to think that it would do so. It is more likely that it would, in the long run, simply broaden the basis for taxation in Iceland, adding yet another source of income to government.

Moreover, there are reasons to believe that such a tax would have distortional effects on operations in the fisheries (Johnson, 1995 and 1999). Consider the possibility that government would gradually take the quotas away from their present holders, over a period of 10 years or so, and rent the quotas again to them, for perhaps 2-3 years. This would mean that the incentives and therefore the behaviour of vessel owners would change. They would no longer think of themselves as having an interest in the long-term productivity of the resource. The responsibility for the resource would lie with government. Therefore, vessel owners might support higher TACs than would be optimal. Monitoring would also become more difficult. One of the great advantages of a ITQ system is that the quota holders each have a well- defined share in the resource; they have an incentive to co-operate amongst themselves and with government, and to monitor harvesting. In short, the difference between the behaviour of vessel owners under an ITQ system and under a system of resource rent taxes is that between owners and tenants.

It may be argued that owners of fishing vessels do not deserve the rent that they will, under the ITQ system, be able to derive from the fish stocks in Icelandic waters. Rent from a natural resource is by definition created not by the firms utilising the resource, but by the limited supply of the resource. In a sense, the generation of vessel owners receiving the initial quotas are indeed enjoying a windfall profit. But it is also the consent and active co-operation of this generation which is crucial to the success of the change in institutions. It is difficult to see any others who deserve the rent, either. It may also be quite difficult to isolate the full rent derivable from a resource in such a way that it will not decrease in the very process of isolating it, as we have seen.

Moreover, if the rent derived from the exclusive access to the fish stocks in Icelandic waters is to be captured by a special resource rent tax, then it would seem only fair that the rent derived from other resources in limited supply, including land, hot springs, and human talent, should also be taxed. This would however be very difficult, both for technical and political reasons. It is by no means certain, either, that a special resource rent tax on the fisheries would make the ITQ system more acceptable to the general public. The most unpopular aspect of the system is that holders of quota can sell it and leave the fisheries with a large sum of money. As the adjustment process goes on, this is likely to happen less and less frequently. More and more people have also become shareholders in fishing firms, as described in Chapter 3. The holders of quotas, although much less vocal than the opponents of the ITQ system, may, in the end, be a much stronger interest group. They have a special interest in the system which is clear and concentrated whereas the interest of each taxpayer in a small share in the revenue from a possible resource rent is rather weak.

What is most important is that when the evolution of the ITQ system is studied, it becomes abundantly clear that it would never have been introduced if it had not been in the interest of owners of fishing capital to accept it. The ITQ system was politically possible, unlike a special resource rent tax or a government auction of quotas, because it did not work against the private interest of vessel owners. It is no worse for that. Economists since Adam Smith have told us that there is nothing wrong with private interest, if and when it coincides with the common good. It is the great advantage of the ITQ system in the fisheries that it directs the private interest of each vessel owner towards the public interest in profitable fisheries and conservation of fish stocks.

Possible Future Developments

If a resource rent tax were imposed on the Icelandic fisheries, it would be a double irony. First, the fisheries problem was that of harmful effects of economic activity. The over-capitalisation and excessive fishing effort, leading to dissipation of the resource rent, was because vessel owners did not operate under an efficient set of rules. The ITQ system enabled them to escape from this 'tragedy of the commons' and to capture the rent previously dissipated. If government then stepped in to remove the rent by a tax, it would have replaced one set of harmful effects for vessel owners, namely rent dissipation in the form of over-capitalisation and excessive fishing effort, with another set of harmful effects, namely the tax. What is the point of legislation if not to make the removal of harmful effects of economic activities possible for those who were, in the first place, affected by those harmful effects?

Second, quite likely much, or even most, revenue from such a tax would be dissipated in the effort by various interest groups to secure a part of it for themselves. Ironically, then, rent dissipation offshore, through the costly process of over-investment in the fisheries, would be replaced with rent dissipation ashore, through the costly process of political redistribution.

Be that as it may, the Icelandic government, in response to the public dissatisfaction with the ITQ system, has appointed two commissions to make suggestions on possible improvements of the ITQ system in the fisheries and on other aspects of resource management in the economy. The work of these two commissions was held up by the court cases on the constitutionality first of the fishing permits and then of the ITQs, mentioned in Chapter 1. But after the decision by the Supreme Court, in the spring of 2000, that the ITQ system was indeed constitutional, the two commissions started deliberating again, probably delivering their final reports in late 2000 or early 2001. It is difficult to predict which recommendations those two commissions will make, and also which, if any, of such recommendations Parliament would accept. The evolution of the ITQ system in New Zealand since its introduction in 1986, in many ways parallel to that in Iceland, may however offer some guidance.

Initially, the New Zealand system differed from the Icelandic one in two important respects. First, vessel catch quotas were issued in terms of tonnes, not fractions of the TAC in each species of fish, the idea being that government would buy or sell quotas to make up for changes in the annual TACs. Secondly, government imposed a resource rent tax on quota holders. Both those measures were later abandoned, and apparently for the same reason, that government felt that closer co-operation with fishing firms was necessary. The quotas became TAC-shares as in Iceland; and a cost recovery charge replaced the resource rent tax (cf. Major, 1999). The rule now applied in New Zealand is that fishing firms bear the full costs of administering and enforcing the ITQ system.

This is also a possible, and indeed quite a likely, outcome of the process of reconciling the general public in Iceland with the ITQ system. If a cost recovery charge were imposed on Icelandic quota holders, presumably they would also get a larger say in the administration and enforcement of the system, which would enhance their sense of responsibility for the resource. It would be an important step towards the self-management of the fisheries and probably also serve to strengthen the rights of quota holders. At present, their rights are imperfect, not only because of the uncertain long-term status of the quotas, but also because those rights are quite narrow in scope, being by definition rights of extraction rather than property. In the near future, the two most important tasks in ITQ fisheries systems will be to find ways of setting TACs in different fish stocks efficiently—not to reach levels of a maximum sustainable yield, but the usually somewhat lower levels of maximum profitability—and to create incentives to increase the value of those fish stocks. These two tasks can only be undertaken by real stakeholders in the fisheries.

One of the main arguments for private property rights is that owners have strong incentives to experiment and innovate in the utilisation of their resources. New techniques in fencing and branding, and in fertilising fishing grounds or genetically improving individual fish, might make fish stocks much more valuable than they are now (De Alessi, 1998). Instead of being hunters and gatherers, fishermen might become cultivators. A process of such experiment and innovation in the fisheries is not likely, however, to take place unless ITQs are strengthened into some forms of legally recognised private property rights.

References

Arnason, R. (1990): 'Minimum Information Management in Fisheries', *Canadian Journal of Economics*, Vol.23, pp.630-53.

Arnason, R. (1994): 'On Catch Discarding in Fisheries', *Marine Resource Economics*, Vol.9, pp.189-208.

Arnason, R. (1996): 'Property Rights as an Organizational Framework in Fisheries: The Cases of Six Fishing Nations', in B. L. Crowley (ed.), *Taking Ownership: Property Rights and Fishery Management on the Atlantic Coast*. Halifax, Nova Scotia: Atlantic Institute for Market Studies, pp.99-144.

Buchanan, J.M. (1959): 'Positive Economics, Welfare Economics, and Political Economy', *Journal of Law and Economics*, Vol.2, pp. 124-38.

Buchanan, J.M. (1997): 'Who Cares Whether the Commons Are Privatized?' *Post-Socialist Political Economy. Selected Essays*, Cheltenham: Edward Elgar, pp.160-7.

Coase, R.H. (1960): 'The Problem of Social Cost', *Journal of Law and Economics*, Vol.3, pp.1-44.

De Alessi, M. (1998): *Fishing for Solutions*. IEA Studies on the Environment No. 11. London: IEA Environment Unit.

Demsetz, H. (1967): 'Toward a Theory of Property Rights', *American Economic Review, Papers and Proceedings*, Vol.57, pp.347-59.

Gissurarson, H.H. (1983): 'The Fish War: A Lesson from Iceland', *The Journal of Economic Affairs*, Vol.3, pp.220-3.

Gissurarson, H.H. (1990): *Fiskistofnarnir vid Island: Thjodareign eda rikiseign?* Reykjavik: Stofnun Jons Thorlakssonar.

Gordon, H.S. (1954): 'The Economic Theory of a Common Property Resource: The Fishery', *Journal of Political Economy*, Vol.62, pp.124-42.

Greenpeace (1997), at
http://www.greenpeace.org/~oceans/index.html.

Gylfason, Thorv. (1990): 'Stjorn fiskveida er ekki einkamal utgerdarmanna', ed. Th. Helgason and O. Jonsson, *Hagsaeld i hufi*, Reykjavik: Haskolautgafan og Sjavarutvegsstofnun Haskolans, pp.120-5.

Hannesson, R. (1994): 'Trends in Fishery Management', ed. E.A. Loyayza, Managing Fishery Resources, World Bank Discussion Paper No. 217.

Hardin, G. (1968): 'The Tragedy of the Commons', *Science*, Vol.62, 13 December, pp. 1,243-8.

Johnson, R.N. (1995): 'Implications of Taxing Quota Value in an Individual Transferable Quota Fishery', *Marine Resource Economics*, Vol.10, pp.327-40.

Johnson, R.N. (1999): 'Rents and Taxes in an ITQ Fishery', in R. Arnason and H.H. Gissurarson (eds.), *Individual Transferable Quotas in Theory and Practice*, pp. 205-13. Reykjavik: University of Iceland Press.

Jonsson, B.B. (1975): 'Audlindaskattur, idnthroun og efnahagsleg framtid Islands', *Fjarmalatidindi*, Vol.22, pp.103-22.

Jonsson, H. (1990): 'Akvardanataka i sjavarutvegi og stjornun fiskveida', *Samfelagstidindi*, Vol.10, pp.99-141.

Libecap, G.D. (1989): *Contracting for Property Rights*, Cambridge: Cambridge University Press.

Lindal, S. (1998): 'Nytjastofnar a Islandsmidum—sameign thjodarinnar', in H.H. Gissurarson et. al. (eds.), *Afmaelisrit David Oddsson fimmtugur*. Reykjavik: Bokafelagid, pp.781-808.

Major, P. (1999): 'The Evolution of ITQs in the New Zealand Fisheries', in R. Arnason and H.H. Gissurarson (eds.), *Individual Transferable Quotas in Theory and Practice*, pp. 81-102. Reykjavik: University of Iceland Press.

Moller, M. (1996): 'Fyrirkomulag veidileyfagjalds', *Visbending*, 29 February.

Morgunbladid (2000): '80% kvotans hafa skipt um hendur', 18 March.

Runolfsson, B. T. (1999): 'ITQs in Iceland: Their Nature and Performance', in R. Arnason and H.H. Gissurarson (eds.), *Individual Transferable Quotas in Theory and Practice*, pp. 103-140. Reykjavik: University of Iceland Press.

Scott, A. (1955): 'The Fishery: The Objectives of Sole Ownership', *Journal of Political Economy*, Vol.63, pp.116-24.

IEA Environment and Technology Programme

Reforming EU Farm Policy: Lessons from New Zealand

R.W.M. Johnson
With a Commentary by Richard Howarth

1. New Zealand is one of the few countries which has embarked on free trade for agriculture.

2. New Zealand farmers were heavily protected by price supports and other measures in the 1970s and early 1980s but protection was greatly reduced in the economic reforms of the mid-1980s.

3. Experience in New Zealand shows that '...agricultural markets do adjust by themselves and that farmers do not bear all the costs of reforms.'

4. Farmers' incomes dropped after the reforms were introduced but farmers then adapted to their new environment. Adjustment in product and factor markets took about six years.

5. Farm land prices fell after the reforms but have now returned to '...a normal relationship with product earnings.'

6. New Zealand would like to see similar reforms in countries whose subsidised output competes with its own. It is also concerned about the growth of 'environmental' obstacles to trade.

7. The Common Agricultural Policy is '...damaging to the interests of consumers and taxpayers in the EU' and burdensome to farmers outside the EU.

8. EU farm protection has been increasing. The 'nominal tariff equivalent' in the EU is now 82 per cent, compared to 1 per cent in New Zealand. The CAP costs a family of four about £1000 per year.

9. The CAP has encouraged higher output and environmental damage. But farmers' incomes have fallen sharply in recent years.

10. Although past EU reform efforts have been ineffective, a '...free market agriculture would be perfectly feasible...'. The New Zealand example should be emulated.

The Institute of Economic Affairs
2 Lord North Street, Westminster, London SW1P 3LB
Telephone: 020 7799 3745 Facsimile: 020 7799 2137
E-mail: iea@iea.org.uk Internet: http://www.iea.org.uk   ISBN 0-255 36484-9

£8.00

WHO, What and Why?

Trans-national Government, Legitimacy and the World Health Organisation

Roger Scruton

1. Trans-national institutions (the United Nations and its affiliates) are increasingly exercising their legislative powers, in order to by-pass the constraints to which national legislatures are subject.

2. The situation is made worse by the habit of conferring leadership of these institutions on ex-politicians, rather than experienced civil servants.

3. Such ex-politicians tend to be more responsive to the concerns of vocal but unrepresentative interest groups, who seek to impose their vision on the people of the world.

4. The World Health Organisation (WHO), after years of blatant corruption and abuse, has been put in the hands of Dr Gro Harlem Brundtland, ex-Prime Minister of Norway.

5. The dangers of this are illustrated by the WHO's 'Tobacco Free Initiative', and its current attempt, eagerly pursued by Dr Brundtland, to secure a draconian Convention against the tobacco industry.

6. The grounds given for this are largely spurious, and in any case refer to matters which are outside the remit of the WHO.

7. The effect of the proposals will be to confer massive legislative and policing powers on unaccountable bureaucrats, and also to drive the trade in tobacco underground.

8. The proposed convention will do nothing to curtail the consumption of tobacco, and everything to escalate the criminal activities of smugglers and rogue producers.

9. The time has come for the WHO to concentrate on its real mission, which is the prevention and cure of communicable diseases such as malaria and TB.

10. Only this will answer the legitimate complaints of those who have seen the Organisation squander millions on projects of little or no relevance to Third-World countries.

The Institute of Economic Affairs

2 Lord North Street, Westminster, London SW1P 3LB
Telephone: 020 7799 3745 Facsimile: 020 7799 2137
E-mail: iea@iea.org.uk Internet: http://www.iea.org.uk

ISBN 0-255 36487-3

£8.00

Fur and Freedom: In Defence of the Fur Trade

Richard D. North
With a Foreword by Roger Scruton

1. Fur farming is no more 'cruel' than many other common farming techniques (such as those used in rearing pigs and chickens).

2. Some consider fur farming morally wrong, but that does not justify banning it. In a pluralistic society such as Britain's, Parliament should encourage toleration, subject to the caveat that people are not harmed. Farming and wearing fur harms nobody.

3. A stronger argument can be made for outlawing the activities of animal liberationists who destroy property and threaten furriers with violence in an attempt to blackmail them into giving up their legitimate trade.

4. The farming of fur is no more unnecessary than the farming of any other animal. We could, in principle, all become vegans, so the farming of animals is not a matter of necessity.

5. Fur farming is not wasteful. Fur farms use waste products from the meat and food industries and turn them into a luxury export.

6. The majority of the world's mink is farmed in Denmark, Holland and the United States. As a proportion of the total, very few are farmed in the UK, so the ban will have almost no effect on the numbers farmed.

7. Whilst fur farming is only a small-scale activity in this country, the fur trade is important to Britain. In fact, the majority of all trade in fur (a trade that was valued at more than £400 million in 1998) is carried on in London.

8. Banning fur farming here would have little immediate effect on this trade but would bolster the spirits of radical anti-fur groups, who might then be encouraged to target the traders. Parliament should think twice before sponsoring such intolerance.

9. 'If new sensitivities emerge and new principles are promulgated, people have a right to see them applied consistently: that is what it means to have equality before the law. That is, if a ban is good for the goose, it is good for the gander too.

10. On such elementary principles we can see that only ill-considered idealism would stigmatise, let alone outlaw, the fur trade and its customers. Public morality is offended by such a ban, with or without compensation for its victims.'

The Institute of Economic Affairs

2 Lord North Street, Westminster, London SW1P 3LB
Telephone: 0171 799 3745 Facsimile: 0171 799 2137
E-mail: iea@iea.org.uk Internet: http://www.iea.org.uk   ISBN 0-255 36486-5

£8.00